GOOD FOOD FOR OUTDOOR ADVENTURES

recipes for eating well
on the trail

Published by Trail Recipes LTD

GOOD FOOD FOR OUTDOOR ADVENTURES

Photographer: All photographs are by the author

ISBN 978-9934-14-869-9

Manufactured in Lithuania

Printed by KOPA® www.kopa.eu

Published by Trail Recipes LTD
www.trail.recipes
info@trail.recipes

contents

You'll love "Good Food For Outdoor Adventures" if you are...

Tired of hauling pounds of food into the backcountry on top of all the equipment required to stay comfortable during the trip;

Fed up with expensive and tasteless commercial food items full of preservatives and other unhealthy additives;

Overwhelmed by the number of ingredients and hard-to-follow cooking instructions included on most backpacking recipes;

Dreading the thought of carrying a whole "kitchen" in your backpack;

Unable to find trail food that suits your dietary needs.

"Good Food For Outdoor Adventures"
will help you to:

Prepare lightweight, quick and delicious meals that you can cook on the trail with minimal gear;

Make muffins, breads and other baked treats in the backcountry;

Start dehydrating food for backpacking meals at home even if you have never done this before;

Plan and organize food for multi-day trip in the wilderness.

In this book, you will find **101 trail-tested recipes** for everything from snacks to desserts as well as tips on food drying methods.

introduction

what food is good for the trail?

Whether you're an experienced outdoorsman, or you're heading out on the trail for the very first time, you need to take the subject of trail food seriously.

The value of good food for outdoor adventures should not be underestimated.

Food gives us the energy essential to keep our bodies going throughout the day and assists with muscle and tissue repair after physical activity. It also keeps us from feeling uncomfortable, which can interfere with our enjoyment and prevent us from focusing on the overall experience.

So, what food is good for the trail? Well, when you're out in the backcountry putting in full days of activity, you want food that is

Delicious - You're going to want food that's tasty.

High-Calorie - You want food that is calorie dense and nutritionally balanced. To have a successful and enjoyable adventure, you need to ensure that your body is optimally fuelled and hydrated.

Lightweight - You need the energy food provides, but you probably won't be hiring a Sherpa to carry it for you. So, you want lightweight meals that can be made on the trail using minimal equipment.

Healthy – You want food that is not only lightweight and tasty, but is also good for you. Most commercially prepared meals are packed with harmful preservatives, salt and sugar. But if you make your own trail meals from scratch, you can control what's going into them and take any of your personal dietary restrictions into account.

Quick - You don't want to wait hours for your meals; you want something that can be cooked quickly, saving you both time and fuel.

Easy - Unless you're an experienced camp chef, you want to have food that is easy to prepare, with simple instructions and ingredients.

No matter what kind of outdoor adventure you're planning, eating well on the trail is the key to success. The recipes in this book have been created to nourish, energize, and revitalize you, all while satisfying your taste buds.

using this book

For clarity and ease of use, each recipe contains information about meal weight, calorie density, cooking time on the trail and the gear required:

Serving size

Most recipes serve 1. Simply scale the quantities up if you are cooking for more.

A few of the snack and dessert recipes provide extra servings so you can share with friends or keep for the next day or two.

Cooking skill levels

Super-Easy – Boiling water is all you need to make your meal

Easy – Cooking isn't an issue, even for amateurs

Moderate – Some cooking skills are required

Cooking time

Time is stated in terms of minutes needed for preparing the meal on the trail.

The cooking times listed on recipes are approximate and could be affected by the weather conditions, altitude, and type of stove you are using.

Calorie density

     Calorie amount per 1 serving

Weight

     The weight of the packed-and-ready-for-the-trail meal is listed in ounces and grams

Cooking gear required

     One Pot – You'll need a single pot to prepare the meal

     Frying Pan – A pan is necessary to prepare the meal

     Pot + Pan – A pot and pan are both needed to prepare the meal

     Outback Oven – You'll need an Outback Oven to prepare the meal

Special diet and food symbols

     Vegetarian – Meatless recipe, ideal for vegetarians

     Vegan – Vegan recipe

     Gluten-Free – Recipe can be used for people who have gluten intolerance

     Spicy food recipe

breakfasts

granola with maple syrup and walnuts

 4　　 5　 431　 93 g / 3.28 oz　　

you'll need:

2 cups rolled oats

1/3 cup shelled walnuts, roughly chopped

2 tablespoons brown sugar

Pinch of sea salt

2 tablespoons canola oil

2 tablespoons maple syrup

8 tablespoons full cream milk powder

at home:

Preheat oven to 160°C / 320°F.

Line a baking sheet with parchment paper.

Combine all ingredients except milk powder in a deep bowl and stir until thoroughly coated.

Place the granola mixture on the baking sheet and roast for 30 minutes until golden brown.

Remove from the oven and let cool completely.

Divide granola into 4 equal portions and pack into separate zip lock bags.

Add to each portion 2 tablespoons of powdered milk and seal the bags.

on the trail:

To make 1 portion:

Pour granola into a bowl.

Add 1/2 cup of hot or cold water; stir well and enjoy.

nutrition (per serving): carbs: **48.1 g**, fat: **22 g**, protein: **11.8 g**, sodium: **135 mg**, sugars: **11.1 g**

granola with hazelnuts, raisins and milk chocolate

 4   5   551   125 g / 4.41 oz

you'll need:

2 cups rolled oats

1/3 cup hazelnuts, roughly chopped

1 tablespoon brown sugar

1/2 teaspoon ground cinnamon

1/4 teaspoon sea salt

2 tablespoons honey

2 tablespoons canola oil

1/2 cup (100 g / 3.5 oz) milk chocolate chips

1/3 cup raisins

8 tablespoons full cream milk powder

at home:

Preheat oven to 160°C / 320°F.

Line a baking sheet with parchment paper.

Combine oats, nuts, sugar, cinnamon, salt, honey and oil in a deep bowl.

Stir until thoroughly coated.

Place the granola mixture on the baking sheet and roast for 30 minutes until golden brown.

Remove from the oven and let cool completely.

Toss milk chocolate and raisins into the granola and mix well.

Divide granola into 4 equal portions and pack into separate zip lock bags.

Add to each portion 2 tablespoons of powdered milk and seal the bags.

on the trail:

To make 1 portion:

Pour granola into a bowl.

Add 1/2 cup of hot or cold water; stir well and enjoy.

nutrition (per serving): carbs: **75.7 g**, fat: **23 g**, protein: **13 g**, sodium: **288 mg**, sugars: **18.6 g**

granola with cranberries and white chocolate

 4   5 485 115 g / 4.06 oz

you'll need:

2 cups rolled oats

1 tablespoon brown sugar

1 teaspoon ground cinnamon

Pinch of sea salt

2 tablespoons canola oil

2 tablespoons honey

1/2 cup white chocolate chips

1/2 cup dried cranberries

8 tablespoons full cream milk powder

at home:

Preheat oven to 160°C / 320°F.

Line a baking sheet with parchment paper.

Combine oats, sugar, cinnamon, salt, canola oil, and honey in a deep bowl. Stir until thoroughly coated.

Place the granola mixture on the baking sheet and roast for 30 minutes until golden brown.

Remove from the oven and let cool completely.

Toss white chocolate and cranberries into the granola and mix well.

Divide granola into 4 equal portions and pack into separate zip lock bags.

Add to each portion 2 tablespoons of powdered milk and seal the bags.

on the trail:

To make 1 portion:

Pour granola into a bowl.

Add 1/2 cup of hot or cold water; stir well and enjoy.

---

nutrition (per serving): carbs: **60.9 g**, fat: **22.1 g**, protein: **11.5 g**, sodium: **153 mg**, sugars: **24.3 g**

coco-nutty granola

 4   5   Cal 463   113 g / 3.99 oz

you'll need:

2 cups rolled oats

1/2 cup sliced almonds

2 tablespoons coconut oil, melted

2 tablespoons agave syrup

2/3 cup unsweetened shredded coconut

8 tablespoons coconut milk powder

at home:

Preheat oven to 160°C / 320°F.

Line a baking sheet with parchment paper.

Combine oats, almonds, coconut oil and agave syrup in a deep bowl.

Stir until thoroughly coated.

Place the granola mixture on the baking sheet and roast for 30 minutes until golden brown.

Remove from the oven and let cool completely.

Toss unsweetened shredded coconut into granola and mix well.

Divide granola into 4 equal portions and pack into separate zip lock bags.

Add to each portion 2 tablespoons of coconut milk powder and seal the bags.

on the trail:

To make 1 portion:

Pour granola into a bowl.

Add 1/2 cup of hot or cold water; stir well and enjoy.

nutrition (per serving): carbs: **43.8 g**, fat: **30.6 g**, protein: **9.5 g**, sodium: **16 mg**, sugars: **2.8 g**

cranberry orange granola

 1   5   506   145 g / 5.11 oz

you'll need:

2 cups rolled oats

1 tablespoon brown sugar

1 teaspoon ground cinnamon

1/4 teaspoon sea salt

Zest of one medium orange

2 tablespoons honey

2 tablespoons canola oil

1 bar (about 100 g / 3.5 oz) dark chocolate (70% cacao), broken into chunks

1/2 cup dried cranberries

8 tablespoons full cream milk powder

at home:

Preheat oven to 160°C / 320°F.

Line a baking sheet with parchment paper.

Combine oats, sugar, cinnamon, salt, orange zest, honey and oil in a deep bowl. Stir until thoroughly coated.

Place the granola mixture on the baking sheet and roast for 30 minutes until golden brown.

Remove from the oven and let cool completely.

Toss dark chocolate and cranberries into granola and mix well.

Divide granola into 4 equal portions and pack into separate zip lock bags.

Add to each portion 2 tablespoons of powdered milk and seal the bags.

on the trail:

To make 1 portion:

Pour granola into a bowl.

Add 1/2 cup of hot or cold water; stir well and enjoy.

nutrition (per serving): carbs: **63.4 g**, fat: **22.7 g**, protein: **12.1 g**, sodium: **212 mg**, sugars: **24.6 g**

superfood granola

 4   5   596   115 g / 4.06 oz   

you'll need:

2 cups puffed quinoa

1/2 cup almonds, roughly chopped

1/2 cup pecans, roughly chopped

1/2 cup dried mulberries

1/4 cup shelled pumpkin seeds (pepitas)

1/4 cup shelled sunflower seeds

2 tablespoons flax seeds

1 tablespoon brown sugar

Pinch of sea salt

2 tablespoons maple syrup

2 tablespoons vegetable oil

8 tablespoons almond milk powder

at home:

Preheat oven to 160°C / 320°F.

Line a baking sheet with parchment paper.

Combine all ingredients except almond milk powder in a deep bowl.

Stir until thoroughly coated.

Place the granola mixture on the baking sheet and roast for 15-20 minutes until golden brown.

Remove from the oven and let cool completely.

Divide granola into 4 equal portions and pack into separate zip lock bags.

Add to each portion 2 tablespoons of almond milk powder and seal the bags.

on the trail:

To make 1 portion:

Pour granola into a bowl.

Add 1/2 cup of hot or cold water; stir well and enjoy.

nutrition (per serving): carbs: **62.2 g**, fat: **34.7 g**, protein: **16.6 g**, sodium: **161 mg**, sugars: **24.3 g**

creamy chocolate buckwheat

 1   10 Cal 541 115 g / 4.06 oz

you'll need:

1/4 cup buckwheat

4 tablespoons full cream milk powder

1 tablespoon dark chocolate baking chips

Pinch of sea salt (optional)

1/4 teaspoon ground cinnamon

1 teaspoon ghee

8–10 pecans, finely chopped

at home:

Grind buckwheat to a powder in a coffee grinder.

Mix ground buckwheat, milk powder, chocolate chips, salt, and cinnamon in a small zip lock bag.

Pack ghee and pecans separately.

on the trail:

Pour the buckwheat mixture into a pot and add in 1 cup water.

Place over medium heat and bring to a boil, stirring occasionally.

Simmer for 2–3 minutes, then remove from the stove and let stand covered for a couple of minutes.

Stir in ghee. Sprinkle with chopped pecans and serve.

nutrition (per serving): carbs: **57.2 g**, fat: **30.6 g**, protein: **16.9 g**, sodium: **539 mg**, sugars: **0.5 g**

sweet coco couscous

 1   10   Cal 359   111 g / 3.92 oz

you'll need:

1/3 cup instant couscous

2 tablespoons coconut milk powder

1 tablespoon unsweetened shredded coconut

1 tablespoon sliced almonds

1 tablespoon dried pineapple chunks, roughly chopped

1 teaspoon brown sugar, or to taste

at home:

Mix all the ingredients in a small zip lock bag.

on the trail:

Bring 1/2 cup water to a boil in a pot.

Remove from the heat and pour in couscous mixture.

Stir well, cover, and let stand for 5 minutes.

Fluff couscous with a spork and enjoy.

nutrition (per serving): carbs: **53.8 g**, fat: **13.9 g**, protein: **8.4 g**, sodium: **13 mg**, sugars: **6.5 g**

peanut butter couscous

 1   10   Cal 513   123 g / 4.34 oz

you'll need:

1/3 cup instant couscous

3 tablespoons full cream milk powder

1 tablespoon sultana raisins

1/8 teaspoon cinnamon powder

1 tablespoon peanut butter

1 tablespoon shelled peanuts, lightly toasted

at home:

Mix couscous, milk powder, raisins and cinnamon in a small zip lock bag.

Pack the remaining ingredients separately.

* Note. To toast shelled peanuts, spread them in an ungreased pan. Bake in a pre-heated oven at 180°C / 350°F for 15–20 minutes, stirring every 5 minutes until golden brown. Remove from the oven and let cool completely.

on the trail:

Bring 1/2 cup water to a boil in a pot.

Remove from the heat and pour in peanut butter and couscous mixture.

Stir well, cover, and let stand for 5 minutes.

Fluff couscous with a spork and enjoy.

nutrition (per serving): carbs: **64.1 g**, fat: **21.4 g**, protein: **19.3 g**, sodium: **188 mg,** sugars: **4 g**

oatmeal with apricots and walnuts

 1   5   Cal 328   77 g / 2.72 oz

you'll need:

1/3 cup quick-cooking oats

2 tablespoons full cream milk powder

1 tablespoon dried apricots, finely chopped

1 teaspoon sugar

1/8 teaspoon ground cinnamon

1 teaspoon ghee

1 tablespoon shelled walnuts, finely chopped

at home:

Mix oats, milk powder, apricots, sugar and cinnamon in a small zip lock bag.

Pack the remaining ingredients separately.

on the trail:

Pour the oat mixture into a bowl.

Add in 1/2 cup hot, boiled water.

Stir well, cover, and let stand for 1 minute.

Stir in ghee; sprinkle with chopped walnuts and enjoy.

nutrition (per serving): carbs: **35.1 g**, fat: **16.9 g**, protein: **10.2 g**, sodium: **74 mg**, sugars: **5.4 g**

nutella and hazelnut oatmeal

 1   5   Cal 318   67 g / 2.36 oz

you'll need:

1/3 cup quick-cooking oats

2 tablespoons full cream milk powder

1 mini-pack (15 g / 0.5 oz) Nutella™ chocolate spread

1 tablespoon toasted hazelnuts, roughly chopped

at home:

Mix oats and milk powder in a small zip lock bag.

Pack the remaining ingredients separately.

* Note: To toast hazelnuts, spread them on ungreased pan or baking sheet. Bake in a pre-heated oven at 180°C / 350°F for 15–20 minutes, stirring every 5 minutes, until lightly browned and skin is blistered. Remove from the oven and let cool completely.

on the trail:

Pour the oat mixture into a bowl.

Add in 1/2 cup hot, boiled water.

Stir well, cover, and let stand for 1 minute.

Stir in the Nutella, sprinkle with hazelnuts, and enjoy.

nutrition (per serving): carbs: **35.8 g**, fat: **15.1 g**, protein: **9.9 g**, sodium: **80 mg**, sugars: **9 g**

crunchy peanut butter oatmeal

 1   5   348   74 g / 2.61 oz

you'll need:

1/3 cup quick-cooking oats

2 tablespoons full cream milk powder

1 tablespoon creamy peanut butter

2 tablespoons crunchy nut granola

at home:

Mix oats and milk powder in a small zip lock bag.

Pack the remaining ingredients separately.

on the trail:

Pour the oat mixture into a bowl.

Add in 1/2 cup hot, boiled water.

Stir well, cover, and let stand for 1 minute.

Stir in peanut butter; sprinkle with granola and enjoy.

nutrition (per serving): carbs: **36.2 g**, fat: **17.3 g**, protein: **13.5 g**, sodium: **154 mg**, sugars: **3.6 g**

oatmeal with bacon, caramelized onions and honey

 1   10 513 108 g / 3.81 oz

you'll need:

1/3 cup quick-cooking oats

2 tablespoons full cream milk powder

Pinch of salt

1 tablespoon ghee

1 small shallot

3 slices shelf-stable bacon

1/2 teaspoon honey, or to taste

at home:

Mix oats, milk powder, and salt in a small zip lock bag.

Pack the remaining ingredients separately.

on the trail:

Pour the oat mixture into a bowl.

Add in 1/2 cup hot, boiled water.

Stir well, cover, and set aside.

Meanwhile, **melt** the ghee in a frying pan over medium heat.

Add the finely chopped shallot and bacon.

Cook together until shallot is soft and caramelized.

Top oatmeal with the shallot and bacon mixture.

Drizzle honey over and serve.

* Variations: Replace honey with maple syrup.

nutrition (per serving): carbs: **33.8 g**, fat: **32.9 g**, protein: **20.2 g**, sodium: **1350 mg**, sugars: **3.2 g**

mango coconut rice pudding

 1   15   Cal 421   120 g / 4.23 oz

you'll need:

1/3 cup quick-cooking rice flakes

1 handful freeze-dried mango chunks

2 tablespoons coconut milk powder

1 teaspoon sugar, or to taste

at home:

Grind rice flakes and mango chunks to a powder in a coffee grinder.

Mix all the ingredients in a small zip lock bag.

on the trail:

Pour the rice pudding mixture into a bowl.

Add in 1/2 cup hot, boiled water.

Stir well, cover, and let stand for 1 minute.

nutrition (per serving): carbs: **78.3 g**, fat: **10.2 g**, protein: **3.8 g**, sodium: **17 mg**, sugars: **44.3 g**

smoked salmon burritos

 1   10   Cal 733   297 g / 10.47 oz

you'll need:

4 tablespoons powdered whole eggs

1 tablespoon full cream milk powder

Salt, to taste

Pepper, to taste

1 teaspoon olive oil

2 medium-sized wheat flour tortillas

1 packet (about 100 g / 3.5 oz) smoked salmon

2 mini packages (each 35 g / 1.25 oz) cream cheese

at home:

Mix powdered eggs and milk powder in a medium-sized zip lock bag.

Pack the remaining ingredients separately.

on the trail:

Pour 1/2 cup water into the bag with the egg mixture.

Beat well with a fork or small whisk.

Season to taste with salt and pepper.

Close the bag and set aside.

Heat the olive oil in a pan over medium-low heat.

Pour in the egg mixture and let it sit, without stirring, for 20 seconds.

Gently **scramble** until the eggs are softly set; then remove from heat.

Spread half of the cream cheese on a tortilla.

Spoon half of the egg mixture over the cheese.

Top with half of flaked smoked salmon.

Roll up the burrito, tucking in its ends.

Repeat with the remaining tortilla.

nutrition (per serving): carbs: **51.7 g**, fat: **38.2 g**, protein: **46 g**, sodium: **2977 mg**, sugars: **2.1 g**

simple scrambled eggs

 1   10   Cal 224   40 g / 1.41 oz

you'll need:

4 tablespoons powdered whole eggs

1 tablespoon full cream milk powder

Salt, to taste

Pepper, to taste

1 tablespoon ghee

at home:

Mix powdered eggs and milk powder in a medium-sized zip lock bag.

Pack the remaining ingredients separately.

on the trail:

Pour 1/2 cup water into the bag with the egg mixture.

Beat well with a fork or small whisk.

Season to taste with salt and pepper. Close the bag and set aside.

Melt the ghee in a frying pan over medium-low heat.

Pour in the egg mixture and let sit, without stirring, for 20 seconds.

Gently **scramble** until the eggs are softly set.

nutrition (per serving): carbs: **6.1 g**, fat: **15.5 g**, protein: **14.4 g**, sodium: **511 mg**, sugars: **2 g**

countryside omelette

 1   10   Cal 394   80 g / 2.82 oz

you'll need:

4 tablespoons powdered whole eggs

1 tablespoon full cream milk powder

Salt, to taste

Pepper, to taste

1 tablespoon ghee

1 small shallot

3 slices shelf-stable bacon or ham

at home:

Mix powdered eggs and milk powder in a medium-sized zip lock bag.

Pack the remaining ingredients separately.

on the trail:

Pour 1/2 cup water into the bag with the egg mixture.

Beat well with a fork or small whisk.

Season to taste with salt and pepper.

Close the bag and set aside.

Meanwhile, **melt** the ghee in a frying pan over medium-low heat.

Add the finely chopped shallot and bacon.

Cook together until shallot is soft and translucent.

Pour in the beaten eggs and cook for a few seconds, until the bottom of the omelette is lightly set.

Ease around the edges of the omelette with a fork and fold it over in half.

Continue to cook until golden brown underneath.

nutrition (per serving): carbs: **8.2 g**, fat: **28.1 g**, protein: **25.8 g**, sodium: **1206 mg**, sugars: **2 g**

pancakes with apples and cinnamon

 1   20   Cal 462   189 g / 6.67 oz

you'll need:

1 cup pancake batter mix

1/3 cup dried apples, finely chopped

1 teaspoon sugar, or to taste

1/2 teaspoon ground cinnamon

1 tablespoon ghee

1 tablespoon honey

10 pecans, roughly chopped

at home:

Combine pancake batter mix, dried apples, sugar, and cinnamon in a medium-sized zip lock bag.

Pack the remaining ingredients separately.

on the trail:

Pour 1/2 cup water into the bag with the pancake batter mixture.

Stir until smooth and close the bag.

Leave the batter to rest for 10 minutes.

Put a frying pan over medium heat and melt half the ghee.

Cut off a corner of the bag and squeeze batter into the pan to form 2 to 3 pancakes.

Let the batter cook for 1-2 minutes until bubbles rise up to the top.

Flip pancakes and cook for another minute until golden on both sides.

Repeat the process with the remaining batter.

Serve pancakes topped with honey and chopped pecans.

nutrition (per serving): carbs: **56.2 g**, fat: **23.8 g**, protein: **7.7 g**, sodium: **2 mg**, sugars: **25.5 g**

pancakes with cranberries and orange zest

 1   20 288  132 g / 4.66 oz

you'll need:

1 cup pancake batter mix

2 tablespoons dried cranberries

1 teaspoon sugar, or to taste

1/2 teaspoon dried orange zest

1 tablespoon ghee

at home:

Combine pancake batter mix, cranberries, sugar, and orange zest in a medium-sized zip lock bag.

Pack the remaining ingredients separately.

on the trail:

Pour 1/2 cup water into the bag with the pancake batter mixture.

Stir until smooth and close the bag.

Leave the batter to rest for 10 minutes.

Put a frying pan over medium heat and melt half the ghee.

Cut off a corner of the bag and squeeze batter into the pan to form 2 to 3 pancakes.

Let the batter cook for 1-2 minutes until bubbles rise up to the top.

Flip pancakes and cook for another minute until golden on both sides.

Repeat the process with the remaining batter.

nutrition (per serving): carbs: **32.5 g**, fat: **13.7 g**, protein: **6.1 g**, sodium: **0 mg**, sugars: **4.5 g**

oatmeal pancakes

 1   20   Cal 420   86 g / 3.03 oz

you'll need:

1/4 cup all-purpose flour

1/4 cup oat flour

2 tablespoons full cream milk powder

1 teaspoon sugar, or to taste

1 tablespoon ghee

at home:

Combine flour, oat flour, milk powder, and sugar in a medium-sized zip lock bag.

Pack ghee separately.

on the trail:

Pour 1/2 cup water into the bag with the oatmeal pancake mixture.

Stir until smooth and close the bag.

Leave the batter to rest for 10 minutes.

Put a frying pan over medium heat and melt half the ghee.

Cut off a corner of the bag and squeeze batter into the pan to form 2 to 3 pancakes.

Let the batter cook for 1-2 minutes until bubbles rise up to the top.

Flip pancakes and cook for another minute until golden on both sides.

Repeat the process with the remaining batter.

nutrition (per serving): carbs: **47.6 g**, fat: **20.1 g**, protein: **11.1 g**, sodium: **73 mg**, sugars: **4.1 g**

savoury pancakes with mushrooms

 1   20   Cal 341   134 g / 4.73 oz

you'll need:

1 cup pancake batter mix

1 small handful dried porcini mushrooms, chopped

1/2 teaspoon dried thyme

Pinch of salt

1 tablespoon ghee

at home:

Combine pancake batter mix, mushrooms, thyme and salt in a medium-sized zip lock bag.

Pack the remaining ingredients separately.

on the trail:

Pour 1/2 cup water into the bag with the pancake batter mixture.

Stir until smooth and close the bag.

Leave the batter to rest for 10 minutes.

Put a frying pan over medium heat and melt half the ghee.

Cut off a corner of the bag and squeeze batter into the pan to form 2 to 3 pancakes.

Let the batter cook for 1-2 minutes until bubbles rise up to the top.

Flip pancakes and cook for another minute until golden on both sides.

Repeat the process with the remaining batter.

nutrition (per serving): carbs: **37.3 g**, fat: **13.8 g**, protein: **11.1 g**, sodium: **156 mg**, sugars: **0 g**

pepperoni and cheese quesadilla

 2   10   459  268 g / 9.45 oz

you'll need:

2 teaspoons olive oil

2 tablespoons tomato paste (tubed)

1 teaspoon dried oregano

2 medium-sized wheat flour tortillas

1 handful (about 60 g / 2.11 oz) grated Cheddar cheese

1 pack (about 70 g / 2.47 oz) sliced pepperoni

at home:

Put the olive oil into a leak-proof container.

Pack the remaining ingredients separately.

on the trail:

Mix tomato paste with 2 tablespoons water and oregano in a mug.

Heat 1 teaspoon of olive oil in a frying pan over medium heat.

Put the tortilla in and reduce heat to low.

Fry on one side, then turn and smear the half of tomato sauce over tortilla.

Sprinkle with half of cheese.

Cook until the cheese is melted, then top it with half of pepperoni.

Fold the tortilla in half, remove from the pan, and cut it into wedges.

Repeat the process with the second tortilla.

nutrition (per serving): carbs: **25.9 g**, fat: **31.1 g**, protein: **20.2 g**, sodium: **911 mg**, sugars: **2.1 g**

snacks

cornflake energy bars

 12   -   163   37 g / 1.31 oz

you'll need:

1 cup pitted dried dates

3 cups cornflakes cereal, slightly crushed

1/2 cup shelled sunflower seeds, unsalted

1/4 cup canola oil

1 bar (about 100 g / 3.5 oz) dark chocolate (70% cacao), broken into chunks

at home:

Line a 25 x 20 cm (8 x 10 inch) baking dish with parchment paper.

Pulse dates in a food processor until you get a sticky paste.

Transfer the date paste into a large bowl.

Add cornflakes, sunflower seeds, and canola oil. Stir until well combined.

Press the cornflake mixture into the prepared baking dish.

Melt the chocolate and pour over, spreading evenly.

Cool to room temperature; then refrigerate about 2 hours, or until firm.

Remove the slab from the baking dish and cut it into 12 bars.

Wrap each bar in waxed paper or aluminium foil.

Store bars in an airtight container in the fridge for up to one month, until you are ready to put them in your backpack.

nutrition (per serving): carbs: **22.5 g**, protein: **1.9 g**, fat: **8.1 g**, sodium: **57 mg**, sugars: **14.5 g**

dried fruit "salami"

 4   -   180   57 g / 2.01 oz

you'll need:

1 cup dried apricots

1/4 cup dried cranberries

1/4 cup shelled pumpkin seeds (pepitas)

at home:

Pulse apricots in a food processor until you get a sticky paste.

Add in the dried cranberries and pumpkin seeds.

Process together until well mixed.

Spread the mixture out into the shape of a sausage on a sheet of plastic wrap. Roll up tightly.

Refrigerate for about 1–2 hours, or until firm.

Store the "salami" in an airtight container in the fridge for up to one month, until you are ready to put it in your backpack.

on the trail:

Slice the "salami" with the sharp knife and enjoy.

nutrition (per serving): carbs: **34.8 g**, protein: **2.8 g**, fat: **3.2 g**, sodium: **1 mg**, sugars: **28.8 g**

no bake energy bites

 10   -   160   34 g / 1.20 oz

you'll need:

1 cup pecans

1 cup pitted dried dates

1/2 cup unsweetened shredded coconut, divided

at home:

Pulse pecans in a food processor until finely chopped.

Add dates and 1/4 cup of shredded coconut.

Process together until you get a sticky paste.

Using a tablespoon, **scoop out** the mixture and shape 10 balls about an inch in diameter.

Roll each ball in the remaining coconut flakes.

Place bites in the freezer to set for at least an hour.

Store in an airtight container in the fridge for up to a week, until you are ready to put them in your backpack.

nutrition (per serving): carbs: **16.4 g**, fat: **11.2 g**, protein: **1.5 g**, sodium: **2 mg**, sugars: **12 g**

puffed amaranth and peanut butter bars

 12   -   314   65 g / 2.29 oz

you'll need:

1 cup pitted dried dates

1 cup puffed amaranth

1/3 cup shelled pumpkin seeds (pepitas), unsalted

1/3 cup shelled sunflower seeds, unsalted

1 cup creamy peanut butter

2 tablespoons virgin coconut oil, melted

1 bar (about 100 g / 3.5 oz) dark chocolate (70% cacao), broken into chunks

1/3 cup unsweetened shredded coconut

at home:

Line a 25 x 20 cm (8 x 10 inch) baking dish with parchment paper.

Pulse dates in a food processor until you get a sticky paste.

Transfer the date paste to a large bowl.

Add puffed amaranth, seeds, peanut butter, and coconut oil.

Stir until well combined.

Press the amaranth-peanut butter mixture into the prepared baking dish.

Melt the chocolate and pour over, spreading evenly.

Dust with coconut flakes.

Cool to room temperature; then refrigerate about 2 hours, or until firm.

Remove the slab from the baking dish, and cut it into 12 bars.

Wrap each bar in waxed paper or aluminium foil.

Store bars in an airtight container in the fridge for up to one month, until you are ready to put them in your backpack.

nutrition (per serving): carbs: **27.8 g**, fat: **20.6 g**, protein: **9.4 g**, sodium: **107 mg**, sugars: **16 g**

spicy roasted nuts and seeds

 8   -   260   47 g / 1.66 oz

you'll need:

1 cup pecans

1/2 cup almonds

1/2 cup cashews

1/2 cup shelled pumpkin seeds (pepitas)

1/3 cup shelled sunflower seeds

1 tablespoon olive oil

1 tablespoon honey

1 tablespoon Chana Masala spice mixture

Pinch of sea salt

at home:

Preheat oven to 190°C / 375°F.

Line a baking sheet with parchment paper.

Combine all the ingredients in a large bowl. Stir until thoroughly coated.

Lay spiced nut and seed mixture on a baking sheet in a single layer.

Roast for about 15–20 minutes, stirring every 5 minutes, until lightly browned.

Remove from the oven and let cool completely.

Divide into equal portions and pack into separate zip lock bags.

nutrition (per serving): carbs: **10.6 g**, fat: **22.6 g**, protein: **7.5 g**, sodium: **91 mg**, sugars: **3.3 g**

soups &
chowders

lentil and bacon soup

 1   20   Cal 290   71 g / 2.50 oz

you'll need:

1 tablespoon quick-cooking red lentils

1/2 teaspoon ground cumin

1/4 teaspoon turmeric powder

1/8 teaspoon chili powder

1/4 vegetable bouillon cube, crushed

1 small shallot

1 clove garlic

1 baby carrot

2 slices shelf-stable bacon

1 tablespoon ghee

at home:

Mix lentils, all dried spices and crushed bouillon cube in a small zip lock bag.

Pack the remaining ingredients separately.

on the trail:

Finely **chop** all vegetables and bacon.

Melt the ghee in a pot over medium-low heat.

Add the vegetables and bacon; cook until shallot is soft and translucent.

Stir in the spices and lentil mixture and heat together for another minute.

Pour in 1 cup water and bring to a boil.

Simmer, stirring occasionally, for about 10 minutes, or until lentils are tender.

nutrition (per serving): carbs: **12.5 g**, fat: **21.7 g**, protein: **11.6 g**, sodium: **630 mg**, sugars: **1 g**

chanterelle and lentil soup

 1   20 261  63 g / 2.22 oz

you'll need:

1 small handful dried chanterelle mushrooms

2 tablespoons quick-cooking red lentils

1 tablespoon instant mashed potatoes

1/2 teaspoon dried thyme

1 tablespoon ghee

1 small shallot

1/4 vegetable bouillon cube

at home:

Put dried mushrooms in a medium-sized zip lock bag.

Mix lentils, mashed potatoes, and thyme in another small zip lock bag.

Pack the remaining ingredients separately.

on the trail:

Pour 1 cup water into the bag with mushrooms. Close the bag and let soak for 5 minutes.

Meanwhile, **melt** the ghee in a pot over medium heat.

Add the finely chopped shallot and cook for 5 minutes until softened.

Pour in the mushrooms together with the water they were soaked in. Bring to a boil.

Add the bouillon cube and lentil–potato mixture.

Simmer, stirring occasionally, for about 10 minutes, or until lentils are tender.

nutrition (per serving): carbs: **24.7 g**, fat: **13.1 g**, protein: **9.7 g**, sodium: **313 mg**, sugars: **0.8 g**

spiced lentil soup with coconut milk

 1   20 338 98 g / 3.46 oz

you'll need:

1 tablespoon ghee

1 small shallot

1 teaspoon yellow Thai curry paste

3 tablespoons coconut milk powder

2 tablespoons quick-cooking red lentils

at home:

Pack all the ingredients separately.

on the trail:

Melt the ghee in a pot over medium-low heat.

Add the finely chopped shallot and cook for 5 minutes until softened.

Stir in the curry paste and heat together for another minute.

Mix coconut milk powder with 1 cup water in a mug.

Pour coconut milk into the pot and bring to a boil.

Add lentils and cook for about 10 minutes, stirring occasionally, until lentils are tender.

nutrition (per serving): carbs: **19.6 g**, fat: **26.7 g**, protein: **7.5 g**, sodium: **145 mg**, sugars: **2 g**

miso soup with tortellini

 1   15 238 68 g / 2.40 oz

you'll need:

2/3 cup dried tortellini, cheese and spinach-filled

1 packet (18 g / 0.63 oz) instant miso soup with wakame

at home:

Pack all the ingredients separately.

on the trail:

Bring 1 cup water to a boil in a pot.

Pour in tortellini and cook until they float to the top.

Remove from the heat, add miso, and stir until paste dissolves completely.

nutrition (per serving): carbs: **35.9 g**, fat: **5.5 g**, protein: **12.4 g**, sodium: **1047 mg**, sugars: **5.2 g**

udon miso

 1   20   Cal 324   114 g / 4.02 oz

you'll need:

1 tablespoon dried sliced shiitake mushrooms

1 teaspoon dried wakame seaweed

1 bundle (about 85 g / 3 oz) udon noodles

1 packet (about 18 g / 0.63 oz) instant miso soup

at home:

Pack all the ingredients separately.

on the trail:

Put the shiitake mushrooms in a pot.

Add in 1 cup water, stir, and let stand for 10 minutes.

Place the pot over medium heat and bring to a boil.

Pour in the wakame seaweed and noodles.

Cook for 3-4 minutes, until noodles are cooked through, but are still firm and al dente.

Remove from the heat, add miso, and stir until the paste dissolves completely.

nutrition (per serving): carbs: **62 g**, fat: **3.2 g**, protein: **15 g**, sodium: **1746 mg**, sugars: **11.4 g**

garlic soup with cheese and croutons

 1   15   194 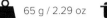 65 g / 2.29 oz

you'll need:

4 garlic cloves

1/2 vegetable bouillon cube

3 tablespoons instant mashed potatoes

Salt, to taste

Pepper, to taste

2 mini-packs (each about 20 g / 0.7 oz) processed cheese

1 tablespoon croutons

at home:

Pack all the ingredients separately.

on the trail:

Put the finely chopped garlic, crushed bouillon cube and instant mashed potatoes into a pot.

Pour in 1 cup water.

Place the pot over medium heat and bring to a boil, stirring occasionally.

Season to taste with salt and pepper.

Simmer for 5 minutes, then remove from the heat and stir in cheese.

Serve topped with croutons.

nutrition (per serving): carbs: **16.3 g**, fat: **10.4 g**, protein: **9.4 g**, sodium: **991 mg,** sugars: **3.7 g**

creamy mushroom soup

 1   15   184   42 g / 1.52 oz

you'll need:

3 tablespoons instant mashed potatoes

2 tablespoons full cream milk powder

1 tablespoon dried and sliced porcini mushrooms

1/2 teaspoon dried thyme

Salt, to taste

Pepper, to taste

1 bay leaf

1 tablespoon croutons (optional)

at home:

Mix mashed potatoes, milk powder, mushrooms, and thyme in a small zip lock bag.

Pack the remaining ingredients separately.

on the trail:

Pour the dry soup mixture into a pot.

Add in 1 cup water, stir well and let stand for 5 minutes.

Place the pot over medium heat and bring to a boil.

Season to taste with salt and pepper.

Put in the bay leaf and simmer, stirring often, for about 5 minutes.

Remove from the heat and discard the bay leaf.

Serve topped with croutons.

nutrition (per serving): carbs: **23.5 g**, fat: **5.9 g**, protein: **8.8 g**, sodium: **250 mg**, sugars: **0 g**

quinoa and sorrel borscht

 1   20   312   85 g / 3 oz

you'll need:

1 portion (about 30 g / 1 oz) beef jerky

1 small shallot

1 baby carrot

1 tablespoon ghee

2 tablespoons quinoa

Salt, to taste

Pepper, to taste

Small bunch of fresh-picked wild sorrel

at home:

Grind beef jerky in a coffee grinder and put it in a small zip lock bag.

Pack the remaining ingredients separately.

on the trail:

Pick and thoroughly wash the sorrel. Peel and dice the vegetables.

Melt the ghee in a pot over medium-low heat.

Add the shallot and carrot; cook for 5 minutes until softened.

Pour in 1 cup water and bring to a boil.

Season to taste with salt and pepper.

Stir in the quinoa and beef jerky.

Simmer, stirring occasionally, until everything is cooked through, for about 10 minutes.

Add sorrel and cook for another 3 minutes.

nutrition (per serving): carbs: **24.6 g**, fat: **15.7 g**, protein: **18.9 g**, sodium: **793 mg**, sugars: **5 g**

harira soup

 1   20   419   138 g / 4.87 oz

you'll need:

1 portion (about 30 g / 1 oz) beef jerky

2 tablespoons quick-cooking rice

2 tablespoons quick-cooking lentils

1 teaspoon all-purpose flour

1/2 teaspoon ground cumin

1/4 teaspoon ground coriander

1/4 teaspoon ground cinnamon

1/4 teaspoon turmeric powder

1/8 teaspoon chili powder

1 tablespoon ghee

1 small shallot

2 tablespoons tomato paste (tubed)

Salt, to taste

at home:

Grind the beef jerky in a coffee grinder.

Mix ground jerky, rice and lentils in a small zip lock bag.

Combine flour and spices in another zip lock bag.

Pack the remaining ingredients separately.

on the trail:

Melt the ghee in a pot over medium heat.

Add the finely chopped shallot and cook for 5 minutes until soft and translucent.

Stir in the tomato paste and spice mixture, heat for another minute.

Pour in 1 cup water and bring to a boil. Season to taste.

Add the rice and jerky mixture.

Simmer for about 10 minutes, stirring occasionally, until rice is cooked through.

nutrition (per serving): carbs: **50.1 g**, fat: **14.6 g**, protein: **23.6 g**, sodium: **956 mg**, sugars: **9.1 g**

lohikeitto – finnish fish soup

 1   15 328 122 g / 4.30 oz

you'll need:

2 tablespoons instant mashed potatoes

2 tablespoons full cream milk powder

1/4 teaspoon fish seasoning

1/4 vegetable bouillon cube, crushed

1 tablespoon ghee

1 small shallot

Salt, to taste

Pepper, to taste

1 bay leaf

1 pouch / can (about 70 g / 2.5 oz) boneless pink salmon

at home:

Mix mashed potatoes, milk powder, fish seasoning, and crushed bouillon cube in a zip lock bag.

Pack the remaining ingredients separately.

on the trail:

Melt the ghee in a pot over medium-low heat.

Add the finely chopped shallot and cook for 5 minutes until soft and translucent.

Stir in the potato–milk mixture and 1 cup water.

Bring to a boil, stirring occasionally.

Season to taste with salt and pepper.

Add in the bay leaf and drained salmon and simmer for a further 5 minutes.

Take the pot off the heat and discard the bay leaf.

nutrition (per serving): carbs: **18.4 g**, fat: **19.8 g**, protein: **18.6 g**, sodium: **664 mg**, sugars: **0 g**

curried ramen bowl

 1   10   436   126 g / 4.44 oz

you'll need:

4 tablespoons coconut milk powder

1 teaspoon yellow curry paste

1 block (about 60 g / 2 oz) ramen noodles

at home:

Pack all the ingredients separately.

on the trail:

Pour coconut milk powder into a pot.

Add in 1 cup water and stir well.

Place the pot over medium heat and bring to a boil.

Stir in the curry paste and ramen noodles.

Cook for 3 minutes, until noodles are cooked through.

nutrition (per serving): carbs: **39.6 g**, fat: **27.2 g**, protein: **8.4 g**, sodium: **1528 mg**, sugars: **2 g**

cullen skink

 2   10   386   157 g / 5.54 oz

you'll need:

2 tablespoons full cream milk powder

1/2 vegetable bouillon cube, crushed

1/4 cup instant mashed potatoes

1 tablespoon ghee

1 small shallot

Salt, to taste

Pepper, to taste

1 pouch (about 100 g / 3.5 oz) smoked haddock or salmon fillet

at home:

Mix the milk powder, bouillon cube, and instant mashed potatoes in a zip lock bag.

Pack the remaining ingredients separately.

on the trail:

Melt the ghee in a pot over medium-low heat.

Add the finely chopped shallot and cook for 5 minutes until soft and translucent.

Stir in the dry soup mixture and 2 cups water.

Bring to a boil and season to taste.

Add flaked fish to the pot and cook for a further 5 minutes, stirring occasionally.

nutrition (per serving): carbs: **19.9 g**, fat: **19.5 g**, protein: **31.6 g**, sodium: **1310 mg,** sugars: **0.7 g**

main courses

green tofu curry

 1　　　　 30　　 Cal 674　　 242 g / 8.54 oz　　　　

you'll need:

1/2 cup quick-cooking rice

1 tablespoon ghee

1 clove garlic

1 pack (about 100 g / 3.5 oz) extra-firm tofu, cubed

1 teaspoon Thai green curry paste

2 tablespoons coconut milk powder

at home:

Pack all the ingredients separately.

on the trail:

For rice:

Cook rice in salted, boiling water for about 10 minutes, or according to package instructions. Drain the water and set aside.

For tofu curry:

Melt the ghee in a frying pan over medium heat.

Add in the finely chopped garlic and tofu; cook until the tofu is golden brown.

Stir in the curry paste and heat for another minute.

In a mug, **combine** coconut milk powder with 1/2 cup water.

Pour coconut milk into a pot and bring to a boil, stirring occasionally.

Reduce heat to low and simmer for about 2 minutes, stirring frequently, until the sauce has slightly thickened.

Serve tofu curry over rice.

nutrition (per serving): carbs: **85.6 g**, fat: **29.3 g**, protein: **18.4 g**, sodium: **650 mg**, sugars: **5.6 g**

orzo al pesto

 1　　 15　Cal 449　 127 g / 4.48 oz　

you'll need:

1 tablespoon pine nuts, lightly toasted

Salt, to taste

1/2 cup orzo pasta

1 tablespoon pesto sauce

2 tablespoons grated Parmesan cheese

at home:

Pack all the ingredients separately.

* Note: To toast pine nuts, heat a non-stick frying pan over medium heat. Add pine nuts and cook, stirring frequently, for about 3 minutes, or until golden. Remove from the heat and leave to cool.

on the trail:

Cook pasta in salted, boiling water until al dente, for about 7–9 minutes, or according to package instructions.

Remove from the heat and drain the water.

Stir in pesto sauce and nuts.

Serve topped with Parmesan.

nutrition (per serving): carbs: **36.8 g**, fat: **25.4 g**, protein: **20.3 g**, sodium: **621 mg**, sugars: **2.1 g**

mushroom orzotto

 1   20   Cal 500   149 g / 5.23 oz

you'll need:

1 small handful dried porcini mushrooms

1 tablespoon ghee

1 small shallot

1/2 cup orzo pasta

Salt, to taste

Pepper, to taste

1/2 teaspoon dried thyme

2 tablespoons grated Parmesan cheese

at home:

Put dried mushrooms in a medium-sized zip lock bag.

Pack the remaining ingredients separately.

on the trail:

Pour 1 cup water into the bag with mushrooms and let soak for 10 minutes.

Meanwhile, **melt** the ghee in a pot over medium-low heat.

Add the finely chopped shallot and cook for 5 minutes until soft and translucent.

Add orzo, mushrooms, and the water they were soaked in. Bring to a boil.

Season to taste with salt and pepper, then toss in the thyme.

Cook, stirring occasionally, for about 10 minutes, or until all the water is absorbed.

Serve topped with grated Parmesan.

nutrition (per serving): carbs: **54.7 g**, fat: **21.2 g**, protein: **22.1 g**, sodium: **457 mg**, sugars: **0 g**

easy cheesy salmon pasta

 1   20 366 204 g / 7.20 oz

you'll need:

1 cup (about 100 g / 3.5 oz) farfalle pasta

1 pouch / can (about 70 g / 2.5 oz) boneless pink salmon

1 teaspoon ghee

2 tablespoons grated Parmesan cheese

at home:

Pack all the ingredients separately.

on the trail:

Cook pasta in salted, boiling water until al dente, for about 7–9 minutes, or according to package instructions.

Remove from the heat and drain the water.

Stir in flaked salmon and ghee.

Serve topped with Parmesan.

nutrition (per serving): carbs: **34.9 g**, fat: **12.6 g**, protein: **27.7 g**, sodium: **508 mg**, sugars: **0 g**

casarecce with chorizo and sun-dried tomatoes

 1   20   677   242 g / 8.54 oz

you'll need:

1 cup (about 100 g / 3.5 oz) casarecce pasta

2 tablespoons sun-dried tomatoes, chopped

1 tablespoon ghee

1 small shallot

50 g / 1.76 oz chorizo

1 tablespoon tomato paste (tubed)

2 tablespoons grated Parmesan cheese

at home:

Pack all the ingredients separately.

on the trail:

Cook pasta in salted, boiling water until al dente, for about 7–9 minutes, or according to package instructions.

Remove from the heat and drain the water.

Melt the ghee in a frying pan over medium heat.

Add the finely chopped shallot and chorizo. **Cook** together until shallot is soft and translucent.

Stir in the sun-dried tomatoes, tomato paste, and 2 tablespoons water.

Cook for another minute together; then remove from the heat.

Add pasta to the pan with the chorizo. **Stir** to coat pasta in the sauce.

Serve topped with Parmesan.

nutrition (per serving): carbs: **50.6 g**, fat: **39.4 g**, protein: **28.9 g**, sodium: **1069 mg,** sugars: **5.5 g**

polenta tirolese

 1   20   584   134 g / 4.73 oz

you'll need:

2 tablespoons full cream milk powder

1/4 chicken bouillon cube, crushed

2 tablespoons instant polenta

2 tablespoons grated Parmesan cheese

1 tablespoon ghee

1 small shallot

3 slices shelf-stable smoked bacon

at home:

Mix the milk powder, bouillon cube, and instant polenta in a small zip lock bag.

Pack the remaining ingredients separately.

on the trail:

For polenta:

Bring 1 cup water to a boil in a pot.

Stream in the polenta mixture, whisking continuously.

Reduce heat to low and simmer for about 5 minutes, stirring regularly, until smooth and thick.

Remove from the heat, stir in Parmesan, cover and set aside.

For topping:

Melt the ghee in a frying pan over medium-low heat.

Add the finely chopped shallot and bacon.

Gently **fry** until shallot is soft and caramelized.

Toss bacon grease with onions over cheesy polenta and enjoy.

nutrition (per serving): carbs: **35.4 g**, fat: **37.4 g**, protein: **28 g**, sodium: **1198 mg**, sugars: **0 g**

mushroom polenta with chorizo chips

 1   15   491   126 g / 4.44 oz

you'll need:

2 tablespoons full cream milk powder

2 tablespoons instant polenta

1 small handful (about 10 g / 0.35 oz) dried porcini mushrooms

1/4 teaspoon vegetable bouillon powder

Salt, to taste

Pepper, to taste

2 tablespoons grated Parmesan cheese

30 g / 1 oz chorizo

1 teaspoon olive oil

at home:

Mix the milk powder, instant polenta, dried mushrooms, and bouillon powder in a small zip lock bag.

Pack the remaining ingredients separately.

on the trail:

For polenta:

Bring 1 cup water to a boil in a pot.

Stream in the polenta mixture, whisking continuously.

Season to taste with salt and pepper.

Reduce heat to low and simmer for about 5 minutes, stirring constantly, until smooth and thick.

Remove from the heat, stir in Parmesan, cover, and set aside.

For topping:

Slice the chorizo 1/8in (3mm) thick.

Heat the olive oil in a pan over medium heat.

Add chorizo slices and cook for about 2 minutes on each side until crisp and golden.

Serve polenta topped with chorizo chips.

nutrition (per serving): carbs: **40.7 g**, fat: **24.1 g**, protein: **26.9 g**, sodium: **1376 mg**, sugars: **0 g**

gnocchi al pesto

 1   15 629 210 g / 7.41 oz

you'll need:

1 tablespoon pine nuts

1 cup dried potato gnocchi

2 tablespoons pesto sauce

2 tablespoons grated Parmesan cheese

at home:

Heat a non-stick frying pan over medium heat. Add pine nuts and cook, stirring frequently, for 3 minutes until golden. Remove from the heat and leave to cool.

Pack all the ingredients separately.

on the trail:

Cook the gnocchi in salted, boiling water for about 2 minutes, or until the dumplings float to the top.

Remove from the heat and drain the water.

Toss gnocchi with pesto until evenly coated.

Serve topped with pine nuts and Parmesan.

nutrition (per serving): carbs: **74.2 g**, fat: **27.3 g**, protein: **21.8 g**, sodium: **1944 mg**, sugars: **2.3 g**

pan-fried gnocchi with sun-dried tomatoes

 1   10 563 202 g / 7.13 oz

you'll need:

3–4 sun-dried tomatoes, chopped

1 cup dried potato gnocchi

1 teaspoon dried oregano

1 tablespoon ghee

1 clove garlic

Salt, to taste

Pepper, to taste

2 tablespoons grated Parmesan cheese

at home:

Mix sun-dried tomatoes, gnocchi, and oregano in a zip lock bag.

Pack the remaining ingredients separately.

on the trail:

Melt the ghee in a frying pan over medium heat.

Add the finely sliced garlic and fry until golden.

Pour in the sun-dried tomato and gnocchi mixture.

Cook until dumplings are slightly brown and crispy.

Season to taste with salt and pepper.

Sprinkle with Parmesan and serve.

nutrition (per serving): carbs: **74.3 g**, fat: **21.4 g**, protein: **18.3 g**, sodium: **1756 mg**, sugars: **0.9 g**

gnocchi carbonara

 1   30   Cal 832   261 g / 9.21 oz

you'll need:

2 tablespoons full cream milk powder

1 teaspoon all-purpose flour

1 cup dried potato gnocchi

1 tablespoon ghee

1 small shallot

3 slices shelf-stable bacon

Salt, to taste

Pepper, to taste

2 tablespoons grated Parmesan cheese

at home:

Mix milk powder and flour in a small zip lock bag.

Pack the remaining ingredients separately.

on the trail:

For gnocchi:

Cook the gnocchi in salted, boiling water for about 2 minutes, or until dumplings float to the top.

Remove from the heat and drain the water.

For sauce:

Melt the ghee in a frying pan over medium heat.

Add the finely chopped bacon and shallot.

Cook for 5 minutes until shallot is soft and translucent.

In a mug, **combine** milk mixture with 1/3 cup of cold water.

Pour the milk into a pan with shallots and bacon.

Bring to a boil and season to taste.

Add cooked gnocchi to the pan.

Simmer for about 2 minutes, stirring regularly, until the sauce has thickened.

Serve topped with Parmesan.

nutrition (per serving): carbs: **39.3 g**, fat: **27.3 g**, protein: **34.1 g**, sodium: **2520 mg,** sugars: **0 g**

everybody-can-make pizza

 1   10   Cal 752   269 g / 9.49 oz

you'll need:

3 teaspoons olive oil, divided

2 tablespoons tomato paste (tubed)

1 teaspoon dried oregano

Salt, to taste

2 medium-sized whole wheat flour tortillas

2 handfuls (about 100 g / 3.5 oz) grated Cheddar cheese

1 pack (about 30 g / 1 oz) shelf-stable sliced pepperoni

at home:

Put the olive oil into a leak-proof container.

Pack the remaining ingredients separately.

on the trail:

In a mug, **mix** tomato paste with 1 teaspoon of olive oil, 2 tablespoons of water, and oregano. Season to taste.

Heat 1 teaspoon of olive oil in a frying pan over medium heat.

Put the tortilla in and reduce heat to low.

Smear the half of tomato sauce over tortilla. Top with half of cheese and half of pepperoni.

Cook until the cheese has melted; then remove tortilla from the pan.

Repeat the process with the second tortilla.

nutrition (per serving): carbs: **48.9 g**, fat: **44.5 g**, protein: **38.7 g**, sodium: **1595 mg**, sugars: **6.5 g**

pizza deliziosa

 2   10   627   417 g / 14.71 oz

you'll need:

3 teaspoons olive oil, divided

2 tablespoons tomato paste (tubed)

1 teaspoon dried oregano

Salt, to taste

2 medium-sized whole wheat flour tortillas

2 handfuls (about 100 g / 3.5 oz) grated Cheddar cheese

1 pack (about 70 g / 2.47 oz) shelf-stable sliced pepperoni

1 can (about 114 g / 4 oz) diced peaches in light syrup, drained

at home:

Put the olive oil into a leak-proof container.

Pack the remaining ingredients separately.

on the trail:

In a mug, **mix** tomato paste with 1 teaspoon of olive oil, 2 tablespoons of water, and oregano. Season to taste.

Heat 1 teaspoon of olive oil in a frying pan over medium heat.

Put the tortilla in and reduce heat to low.

Smear half of tomato sauce over tortilla. Top with half of cheese and half of pepperoni and peaches.

Cook until the cheese has melted; then remove tortilla from the pan.

Repeat the process with the second tortilla.

nutrition (per serving): carbs: **59.8 g**, fat: **44.8 g**, protein: **39.7 g**, sodium: **1595 mg**, sugars: **16 g**

beef tagine with dried fruits

 1   15   433   200 g / 7.05 oz

you'll need:

1/3 cup couscous

1 teaspoon ground cumin

1 teaspoon ground cinnamon

1 teaspoon dry brown gravy mix

3 dried apricots, chopped

2 dried prunes, chopped

1 can (about 100 g / 3.5 oz) boneless beef chunks

Salt, to taste

Pepper, to taste

1 tablespoon chopped almonds

at home:

Mix couscous, spices, gravy mix, and dried fruits in a medium-sized zip lock bag.

Pack the remaining ingredients separately.

on the trail:

Bring 1/3 cup water to a boil in a pot.

Stir in the beef chunks and couscous mixture.

Season to taste, then remove from the heat, cover and let stand for 5 minutes.

To serve, **fluff** couscous with a spork and top with chopped almonds.

---

nutrition (per serving): carbs: **72.5 g**, fat: **10.7 g**, protein: **13.8 g**, sodium: **865 mg**, sugars: **10.4 g**

cottage pie

 1   20   Cal 302   162 g / 5.71 oz

you'll need:

1 tablespoon ghee

1 small shallot

1–2 baby carrots

1 can (about 100 g / 3.5 oz) boneless beef chunks

1/2 tablespoon dry brown gravy mix

1 serving (about 1/2 cup) instant mashed potatoes

at home:

Pack all the ingredients separately.

on the trail:

For mashed potatoes:

Pour hot, boiling water into mashed potato mixture. Stir until well combined and set aside.

For gravy:

Melt the ghee in a frying pan over medium-low heat.

Add the finely chopped shallot and carrots. Cook for 5 minutes until softened.

Stir in the beef chunks and heat for another minute.

In a mug, **combine** gravy mix with 1/2 cup of cold water.

Pour gravy into the pan.

Reduce heat to low and simmer for 2 minutes, stirring frequently, until the sauce has thickened.

Serve beef chunks with gravy over mashed potatoes.

nutrition (per serving): carbs: **31.4 g**, fat: **17.3 g**, protein: **6.3 g**, sodium: **601 mg**, sugars: **3.1 g**

mushroom stroganoff

 1   20   Cal 342   80 g / 2.82 oz

you'll need:

1 tablespoon full cream milk powder

1 teaspoon all-purpose flour

1/2 teaspoon thyme

2 tablespoons dried porcini mushrooms

1 tablespoon ghee

1 small shallot

Salt, to taste

Pepper, to taste

1 serving (about 1/2 cup) instant mashed potatoes

at home:

Mix the powdered milk, flour, thyme, and porcini mushrooms in a medium-sized zip lock bag.

Pack the remaining ingredients separately.

on the trail:

For stroganoff:

Pour 1/2 cup water into the bag with the mushroom mixture.

Stir well, close the bag and let stand for 10 minutes.

Meanwhile, **melt** the ghee in a frying pan over medium-low heat.

Add the finely chopped shallot and cook until soft and translucent.

Add mushrooms together with the liquid they were soaked in to the pan.

Bring to a boil and season to taste.

Reduce heat to low and simmer for about 2 minutes, stirring regularly, until the sauce has thickened.

For mashed potatoes:

Pour hot, boiling water into mashed potato mixture. Stir until well combined and set aside.

Serve mushroom stroganoff over mashed potatoes.

nutrition (per serving): carbs: **37.5 g**, fat: **15.7 g**, protein: **10 g**, sodium: **218 mg**, sugars: **0.8 g**

moroccan spiced tuna couscous

 1   10   435   190 g / 6.70 oz

you'll need:

1/3 cup couscous

2 tablespoons sun-dried tomatoes, chopped

1 teaspoon Ras-el-Hanout (tagine spice mixture)

2 tablespoons tomato paste

Salt, to taste

1 can / pouch (about 75 g / 2.5 oz) tuna in oil

at home:

Mix couscous, sun-dried tomatoes, and Ras-el-Hanout spice blend in a medium-sized zip lock bag.

Pack the remaining ingredients separately.

on the trail:

Bring 1/3 cup water to a boil in a pot.

Stir in the couscous mixture and tomato paste.

Season to taste, then remove from the heat, cover and let stand for 5 minutes.

To serve, **fluff** couscous with a spork and top with tuna pieces.

nutrition (per serving): carbs: **60 g**, fat: **10.2 g**, protein: **25.5 g**, sodium: **540 mg**, sugars: **3.9 g**

goulash with mashed potatoes

 1   20   Cal 328   188 g / 6.63 oz

you'll need:

1 serving (about 1/2 cup) instant mashed potatoes

1 tablespoon ghee

1 small shallot

1 clove garlic

2 tablespoons tomato paste (tubed)

1 teaspoon Hungarian sweet paprika powder

1 can (about 100 g / 3.5 oz) boneless beef chunks

Salt, to taste

Pepper, to taste

at home:

Pack all the ingredients separately.

on the trail:

For mashed potatoes:

Pour hot, boiling water into mashed potato mixture. Stir until well combined and set aside.

For goulash:

Melt the ghee in a frying pan over medium-low heat.

Add the finely chopped shallot and garlic.

Gently **fry** for about 3 minutes, stirring regularly.

Stir in the tomato paste, paprika and beef chunks. Heat for another minute.

Pour in 1/2 cup water. Bring to a boil and season to taste.

Simmer, stirring occasionally, for about 5 minutes, then remove from heat.

Serve goulash over mashed potatoes.

nutrition (per serving): carbs: **38.9 g**, fat: **22.1 g**, protein: **7.9 g**, sodium: **485 mg**, sugars: **5.6 g**

fish crumble

 2   20   Cal 359   312 g / 11 oz

you'll need:

2 tablespoons full cream milk powder

2 teaspoons all-purpose flour

1 teaspoon fish seasoning

2 tablespoons grated Parmesan cheese

1 tablespoon bread crumbs

2 servings (about 1 cup) instant mashed potatoes

1 tablespoon ghee

1 small shallot

Salt, to taste

Pepper, to taste

1 pouch / can (about 75 g / 2.5 oz) boneless pink salmon

1 pouch (about 100 g / 3.5 oz) imitation crab meat

at home:

Mix the powdered milk, flour, and fish seasoning in a small-sized zip lock bag. **Combine** grated Parmesan cheese and breadcrumbs in another bag.

Pack the remaining ingredients separately.

on the trail:

For mashed potatoes:

Pour hot, boiling water into mashed potato mixture. Stir until well combined and set aside.

For fish sauce:

Melt the ghee in a pan over medium heat.

Add the finely chopped shallot and cook until soft and translucent.

In a mug, **combine** the milk and flour mixture with 2/3 cup of cold water. **Fold** milk into the pan and bring to a boil, stirring occasionally.

Season to taste with salt and pepper.

Add in the drained salmon and crab meat. Cook together for another minute until the sauce has thickened.

To assemble the meal:

Spoon mashed potatoes over the fish sauce and spread evenly.

Sprinkle cheese and breadcrumb mixture on the mashed potatoes to serve.

nutrition (per serving): carbs: **38.7 g**, fat: **13.6 g**, protein: **20.7 g**, sodium: **1003 mg**, sugars: **4.2 g**

smoked sausage jambalaya

 1   20   Cal 512  183 g / 6.46 oz

you'll need:

1 tablespoon ghee

1 small shallot

1 garlic clove

1 pack (about 50 g / 1.75 oz) sliced summer sausage or shelf-stable salami

2–3 canned pimentos, diced

1 tablespoon tomato paste (tubed)

1/2 teaspoon Cajun spice mixture

1/3 cup quick-cooking rice

Salt, to taste

at home:

Pack all the ingredients separately.

on the trail:

Melt the ghee in a pot over medium heat.

Add the finely chopped shallot, garlic, and smoked sausage.

Gently **fry** until shallot is soft and golden.

Stir in the pimentos, tomato paste, and Cajun spice mixture.

Cook for another 1–2 minutes.

Pour in the rice and 2/3 cup water. Bring to a boil and season to taste.

Simmer for about 10 minutes, stirring regularly, until the rice is done and almost all the liquid is absorbed.

nutrition (per serving): carbs: **57.7 g**, fat: **24.8 g**, protein: **13.8 g**, sodium: **652 mg**, sugars: **4.2 g**

black mountain paella

 2   25 510 450 g / 15.87 oz

you'll need:

1 tablespoon olive oil

1 pack (about 50 g / 1.75 oz) sliced chorizo or summer sausage

1 shallot

2 garlic cloves

2 tablespoons tomato paste (tubed)

1/2 teaspoon sweet smoked paprika

1 packet (4 g / 0.14 oz) squid ink

1/2 vegetable bouillon cube

Salt, to taste

2/3 cup paella rice

1 can (about 85 g / 3 oz) smoked mussels

1 can (about 100 g / 3.5 oz) squid in ink

at home:

Pack all the ingredients separately.

on the trail:

Heat the olive oil in a pot over medium heat.

Add the chorizo and cook, stirring, for 3–4 minutes until crisp.

Add the finely chopped shallot and garlic. Cook until shallot is soft and golden.

Stir in the tomato paste, paprika, and squid ink; distribute evenly.

Pour in the rice and 1-1/2 cup water.

Bring to a boil and crumble in the bouillon cube.

Season to taste and simmer for 10 minutes.

Stir in the drained seafood and cook for another 5 minutes together until the rice is done and almost all the liquid is absorbed.

nutrition (per serving): carbs: **49.9 g**, fat: **24.8 g**, protein: **20.8 g**, sodium: **1306 mg**, sugars: **4.3 g**

quinoa and crab curry

 1   20   424   181 g / 6.38 oz

you'll need:

1 tablespoon ghee

1 teaspoon yellow curry paste

2 tablespoons coconut milk powder

3 tablespoons quinoa

1 pouch (about 100 g / 3.5 oz) imitation crab meat

at home:

Pack all the ingredients separately.

on the trail:

Melt the ghee in a pot.

Add the curry paste and heat for another minute.

In a mug, **combine** coconut milk powder with 1 cup water.

Pour milk into the pot and bring to a boil.

Add in rinsed and drained quinoa.

Simmer, stirring occasionally, until the quinoa is cooked through.

Add the crab meat and cook for a further couple of minutes.

Enjoy with wheat tortilla or chapati. (See how to make chapati on page 126)

nutrition (per serving): carbs: **38.1 g**, fat: **25.3 g**, protein: **12.9 g**, sodium: **982 mg**, sugars: **7.2 g**

tuna curry with rice

 1   20 682 150 g / 5.29 oz

you'll need:

1 tablespoon ghee

1 small shallot

1 tablespoon Thai yellow curry paste (or 1 teaspoon mild curry powder)

4 tablespoons powdered coconut milk

1/3 cup quick-cooking rice

Salt, to taste

1 can or pouch (about 70 g / 2.47 oz) tuna chunks in water, drained

at home:

Pack all the ingredients separately.

on the trail:

Melt the ghee in a pot over medium-low heat.

Add the finely chopped shallot and cook until soft and translucent.

Stir in the curry paste (or curry powder) and heat for another minute.

In a mug, **combine** coconut milk powder with 1 cup water.

Pour the coconut milk along with the rice into the pot.

Bring to a boil and season, if desired.

Simmer for another 10 minutes, stirring occasionally, until the rice is done and almost all the liquid is absorbed.

Remove from the heat, stir in tuna pieces and serve.

nutrition (per serving): carbs: **61 g**, fat: **39.2 g**, protein: **21.5 g**, sodium: **437 mg**, sugars: **2.1 g**

bulgur pilaf

 1   20   Cal 411   160 g / 5.64 oz

you'll need:

1/2 cup quick-cooking bulgur

1/8 teaspoon chili powder

1/2 teaspoon ground cumin

1/2 teaspoon sweet paprika powder

1 tablespoon ghee

1 shallot

2 tablespoons tomato paste (tubed)

3-4 canned pimentos

Salt, to taste

Pepper, to taste

at home:

Mix the bulgur, chili powder, cumin, and paprika in a zip lock bag.

Pack the remaining ingredients separately.

on the trail:

Melt the ghee in a pot over medium heat.

Add the finely chopped shallot and cook until soft and translucent.

Stir in the tomato paste, sliced pimentos, and the bulgur-spice mixture.

Heat together for 1 minute.

Pour in 1 cup water and bring to a boil. Season.

Simmer for another 6–7 minutes, stirring occasionally, until the bulgur is cooked through and almost all the liquid is absorbed.

nutrition (per serving): carbs: **65.3 g**, fat: **17.2 g**, protein: **10.8 g**, sodium: **206 mg**, sugars: **5.5 g**

turkey with cranberry gravy and mashed sweet potatoes

 1   15   376   216 g / 7.62 oz

you'll need:

1 tablespoon dry gravy mix

2 tablespoons dried cranberries

Pinch of dried rosemary

1 serving (about 1/2 cup) sweet mashed potatoes

1 pouch / can (about 140 g / 5 oz) turkey breast

at home:

Combine the gravy mix, dried cranberries, and rosemary in a small zip lock bag.

Pack the remaining ingredients separately.

on the trail:

For mashed potatoes:

Pour hot, boiling water into mashed potato mixture. Stir until well combined and set aside.

For gravy:

In a mug, **combine** the gravy mix with 1/3 cup of cold water.

Pour gravy into a pan and bring to a boil, stirring.

Add turkey and simmer together for another 2 minutes, stirring continuously, until the gravy has thickened.

Serve turkey and gravy over mashed potatoes.

nutrition (per serving): carbs: **19.8 g**, fat: **10.2 g**, protein: **42 g**, sodium: **533 mg,** sugars: **7.3 g**

wasabi fish cakes

 1   20 Cal 286 110 g / 3.88 oz

you'll need:

2 tablespoons potato pancake mix

1/2 teaspoon wasabi powder

1 can / pouch (about 75 g / 2.5 oz) tuna in oil

Salt, to taste

Pepper, to taste

1 teaspoon olive oil

at home:

Combine the potato pancake mix and wasabi powder in a medium-sized zip lock bag.

Pack the remaining ingredients separately.

on the trail:

Pour 1/4 cup of cold water into the bag with the potato pancake and wasabi mixture.

Add the drained and flaked tuna. Season to taste and stir until well combined.

Heat the olive oil in a frying pan.

Spoon the fish cake mixture into the pan to form 4 small patties.

Cook fish cakes on both sides until golden brown.

Enjoy by itself or served over rice, noodles, or mashed potatoes.

nutrition (per serving): carbs: **14.6 g**, fat: **19 g**, protein: **16.1 g**, sodium: **736 mg**, sugars: **0.7 g**

poached trout

 1   20   Cal 405   57 g / 2.01 oz

you'll need:

1 fresh-caught trout, cleaned and head removed

Salt, to taste

Pepper, to taste

2 bay leaves

1 shallot, sliced

1/2 lemon, divided

Pinch of dried thyme

1 tablespoon ghee

on the trail:

Cut the fish in half or into steaks to fit the pot.

Season with salt and pepper.

Set the fish in the pot; add bay leaves.

Lay onion rings and 2–3 lemon slices over the fish. Sprinkle with thyme.

Add enough cold water just to cover the fish.

Bring to a boil, and then simmer uncovered for 6 minutes.

Remove from the heat and take the trout out of the pot.

Serve with ghee and lemon wedges.

nutrition (per serving): carbs: **7.6 g**, fat: **23.2 g**, protein: **40.9 g**, sodium: **158 mg**, sugars: **0.8 g**

chapati

 4   30   183   160 g / 5.64 oz

you'll need:

1 cup all-purpose flour, plus extra for kneading

1 tablespoon full cream milk powder

Pinch of salt

Ghee for brushing

at home:

Mix the flour, milk powder, and salt in a medium-sized zip lock bag.

Pack the ghee separately.

on the trail:

Pour 1/3 cup water (or more, if needed) into the bag with the flour mixture.

Close the bag and knead the smooth dough.

Leave to rest for about 5 minutes.

Divide the dough into 8 parts.

Shape each piece into a ball, then roll out or knead into flat disks (as thin as possible).

Place a pan over medium heat.

Fry the chapati one at a time, for 1-2 minutes on both sides or until golden-brown.

Take out of the pan and brush with ghee.

Serve with curries, spicy couscous, and soups.

nutrition (per serving): carbs: **24.9 g**, fat: **7.4 g**, protein: **3.9 g**, sodium: **49 mg**, sugars: **0 g**

desserts

wild berry soup

 1   10 118 6 g / 0.21 oz

you'll need:

1 cup fresh-picked wild berries (raspberries, blueberries)

1 teaspoon sugar, or to taste

1 teaspoon potato starch

on the trail:

Place the berries into a pot, add 1/2 cup water and bring to a boil.

Stir in the sugar and simmer on a low heat for 5 minutes.

Mix the potato starch with a little cold water in a mug.

Take the pot off the heat and stir in the potato-starch mixture.

Return to a gentle heat, stirring continuously until the soup has slightly thickened. Do not let the mixture boil after adding the potato starch.

Serve warm or cold.

nutrition (per serving): carbs: **30 g**, fat: **0.5 g**, protein: **1.1 g**, sodium: **2 mg**, sugars: **18.7 g**

sun-rice pudding

 1   10   596   165 g / 5.82 oz

you'll need:

4 tablespoons coconut milk powder

1 tablespoon full cream milk powder

1 teaspoon brown sugar, or to taste

1/4 teaspoon ground cardamom

1/3 cup quick-cooking rice flakes

1 tablespoon raisins

1 tablespoon sliced almonds

1 tablespoon pistachio nuts, chopped

at home:

Mix the coconut milk powder, milk powder, sugar, and cardamom in a small zip lock bag.

Pack the remaining ingredients separately.

on the trail:

Pour the dry milk mixture into a pot.

Add in 1 cup water and bring to a boil.

Stir in the rice flakes and raisins.

Reduce heat to low and simmer, stirring frequently, until the mixture has thickened.

To serve, **garnish** with almonds and pistachios.

nutrition (per serving): carbs: **65.4 g**, fat: **31.9 g**, protein: **14.2 g**, sodium: **47 mg**, sugars: **14.9 g**

banana in coconut milk

 1   20   530   167 g / 5.89 oz

you'll need:

3 tablespoons coconut milk powder

1 teaspoon brown sugar, or to taste

Small pinch of sea salt (optional)

1 just ripe banana (not overripe)

at home:

Mix the coconut milk powder, sugar, and sea salt in small zip lock bag.

Pack the banana separately.

on the trail:

Pour the coconut milk mixture into a pot.

Add in 3/4 cup water and bring to a boil.

Peel the banana and cut into 5 cm (2 inch) lengths.

Add the banana to the pot.

Simmer, stirring occasionally, for about 4–5 minutes, or until banana is soft.

Allow to cool slightly before serving.

nutrition (per serving): carbs: **39.9 g**, fat: **43.3 g**, protein: **5.4 g**, sodium: **263 mg**, sugars: **23.4 g**

easy trail tiramisu

 1   20   492    141 g / 4.97 oz

you'll need:

1 tablespoon vanilla custard powder

3 tablespoons full cream milk powder

1 teaspoon sugar

1 tablespoon amaretto almond liquor

1 teaspoon instant coffee

6 pcs ladyfinger biscuits

1 teaspoon cacao powder

at home:

Mix the vanilla custard powder, milk powder, and sugar in a small zip lock bag.

Put the amaretto liqour in a small leak-proof container.

Pack the remaining ingredients separately.

on the trail:

In a mug, **mix** instant coffee with 1/4 cup of hot, boiled water. Set aside.

Pour the vanilla custard mixture into a pot and gradually add 3/4 cup of cold water.

Place the pot over medium heat and bring to a boil, stirring continuously.

Reduce the heat to low and simmer for at least one minute until the custard has thickened. Then, immediately remove from the stove and leave to cool.

Stir in the amaretto liquor.

Add half of the crushed biscuits into the mug. Drizzle with half the coffee.

Spread half the vanilla custard over ladyfingers.

Repeat the layers.

Dust with cocoa powder and serve.

nutrition (per serving): carbs: **72.7 g**, fat: **16 g**, protein: **13.1 g**, sodium: **255 mg**, sugars: **28.1 g**

very berry no bake crumble

 1   10  328 61 g / 2.15 oz

you'll need:

1 cup fresh-picked wild berries (blueberries, raspberries, blackberries)

1 tablespoon sugar, or to taste

1/2 cup crunchy granola

on the trail:

Pour wild berry mixture into a pot and toss with the sugar.

Place the pot over medium-low heat and cook, stirring constantly, until the sugar is melted and mixture has thickened.

Sprinkle crunchy granola over the berries and enjoy.

nutrition (per serving): carbs: **68 g**, fat: **4.5 g**, protein: **8.1 g**, sodium: **1 mg**, sugars: **32.4 g**

chocolate pudding trifle

 1   20 374 80 g / 2.82 oz

you'll need:

2 tablespoons instant chocolate pudding

2 tablespoons full cream milk powder

1 teaspoon sugar

4 amaretti biscuits, crushed

1 tablespoon hazelnuts, lightly toasted and roughly chopped

at home:

Mix the instant chocolate pudding, sugar, and milk powder in a small zip lock bag.

Pack the remaining ingredients separately.

on the trail:

Pour the chocolate pudding mixture into a pot.

Add in 1 cup water and bring to a gentle boil, stirring frequently.

Remove from the heat and set aside to cool.

Pour half of the pudding into a mug.

Add a layer of crushed amaretti biscuits.

Cover with the rest of the pudding and sprinkle with chopped hazelnuts to serve.

nutrition (per serving): carbs: **54.8 g**, fat: **12.5 g**, protein: **7.7 g**, sodium: **512 mg**, sugars: **24.2 g**

drinks

dried fruit compote

 1   15   215   84 g / 2.96 oz

you'll need:

1/2 cup dried fruit mix (prunes, apricots, figs, peaches)

2 whole cloves

1 cinnamon stick

1 teaspoon sugar, or to taste

at home:

Mix all the ingredients in a small zip lock bag.

on the trail:

Bring 1 cup water to a boil in a pot.

Pour in the dried fruits, spices, and sugar.

Reduce heat to medium-low and simmer, stirring occasionally, for 5 minutes.

Remove from the heat and let stand covered for another 5 minutes.

Allow to cool slightly before serving.

nutrition (per serving): carbs: **54 g**, fat: **0 g**, protein: **2 g**, sodium: **120 mg**, sugars: **38 g**

masala chai

 1　　 10　 124　 31 g / 1.09 oz　

you'll need:

2 tablespoons full cream milk powder

1/4 teaspoon ground cardamom

1/8 teaspoon ground ginger

1/4 teaspoon ground cinnamon

1/8 teaspoon ground cloves

1 teaspoon sugar, or to taste

1 teabag black tea

at home:

Mix the powdered milk, spices, and sugar in a small zip lock bag.

Pack the teabag separately.

on the trail:

Pour the milk mixture and 1 cup water into a pot. Stir well.

Bring to a boil, then remove from the heat and add the teabag.

Cover and let steep for 3 minutes.

nutrition (per serving): carbs: **13.2 g**, fat: **5.7 g**, protein: **4.9 g**, sodium: **73 mg**, sugars: **4 g**

cocoa drink

 1   5   123   26 g / 0.92 oz

you'll need:

2 tablespoons full cream milk powder

1 teaspoon cocoa powder

1 teaspoon sugar, or to taste

at home:

Mix all the ingredients in a small zip lock bag.

on the trail:

Bring 1 cup water to a boil.

Pour the cocoa mixture into a mug.

Add 2 tablespoons of hot water and mix to a smooth paste.

Add the rest of the water and whisk for 20 seconds.

nutrition (per serving): carbs: **13 g**, fat: **5.8 g**, protein: **5.1 g**, sodium: **72 mg**, sugars: **4 g**

really hot chocolate

 1   5   199   42 g / 1.48 oz

you'll need:

1 teaspoon cocoa powder

2 teaspoons sugar

1 tablespoon grated dark chocolate

2 tablespoons full cream milk powder

1/2 teaspoon corn flour

Pinch of salt

Small pinch of cayenne pepper

at home:

Mix all the ingredients in a small zip lock bag.

on the trail:

Bring 1 cup water to a boil.

Pour the chocolate mixture into a mug.

Add 2 tablespoons of hot water and mix to a smooth paste.

Add the rest of the water and whisk for 20 seconds.

nutrition (per serving): carbs: **24.2 g**, fat: **9 g**, protein: **6 g**, sodium: **236 mg**, sugars: **13.4 g**

pina colada latte

 1   5 206  40 g / 1.41 oz

you'll need:

2 tablespoons coconut milk powder

1 teaspoon full cream milk powder

1/2 teaspoon cocoa powder

1 teaspoon instant coffee

1 teaspoon sugar, or to taste

at home:

Mix all the ingredients in a small zip lock bag.

on the trail:

Bring 1 cup water to a boil.

Pour the pina colada latte mixture into a mug.

Add 2 tablespoons of hot water and mix to a smooth paste.

Add the rest of the water and whisk for 20 seconds.

nutrition (per serving): carbs: **13.5 g**, fat: **15.33 g**, protein: **4 g**, sodium: **60 mg**, sugars: **5.4 g**

halva coffee

 1   5 266 51 g / 1.80 oz

you'll need:

1 tablespoon (about 30 g / 1 oz) peanut halva

2 tablespoons full cream milk powder

1 teaspoon instant coffee

at home:

Grind halva in a coffee grinder.

Mix halva, powdered milk and coffee in a small zip lock bag.

on the trail:

Bring 1 cup water to a boil.

Pour the halva coffee mixture into a mug.

Add 2 tablespoons of hot water and mix to a smooth paste.

Add the rest of the water and whisk for 20 seconds.

nutrition (per serving): carbs: **25.4 g**, fat: **14.6 g**, protein: **7.9 g**, sodium: **147 mg,** sugars: **9 g**

mocha latte

 1   5   Cal 73   17 g / 0.60 oz

you'll need:

1 tablespoon full cream milk powder

1 teaspoon cocoa powder

1 teaspoon sugar, or to taste

1 teaspoon instant coffee

at home:

Mix all the ingredients in a small zip lock bag.

on the trail:

Bring 1 cup water to a boil.

Pour the mocha latte mixture into a mug.

Add 2 tablespoons of hot water and mix to a smooth paste.

Add the rest of the water and whisk for 20 seconds.

nutrition (per serving): carbs: **9.4 g**, fat: **3 g**, protein: **2.8 g**, sodium: **37 mg**, sugars: **4 g**

after dinner tea

 1   5   Cal 23   13 g / 0.46 oz

you'll need:

1 teaspoon dried chamomile

1 teaspoon dried peppermint

1 teaspoon fennel seeds, crushed

1 empty teabag or muslin bag

1 teaspoon sugar, to taste

at home:

Mix chamomile, peppermint, and fennel seeds.

Put the dried herb mixture in an empty teabag, then pack into a small zip lock bag.

on the trail:

Bring 1 cup water to a boil in a pot.

Take the pot off the heat and put in the teabag.

Let steep for 5 minutes.

Sweeten with sugar if desired.

nutrition (per serving): carbs: **5.2 g**, fat: **0.3 g**, protein: **0.4 g**, sodium: **2 mg**, sugars: **4 g**

good night tea

 1   10   Cal 74   21 g / 0.74 oz

you'll need:

1 tablespoon full cream milk powder

1/8 teaspoon vanilla powder

1 teaspoon sugar, or to taste

1 teabag chamomile tea

at home:

Mix the powdered milk, vanilla, and sugar in a small zip lock bag.

Pack the teabag separately.

on the trail:

Pour the vanilla-milk mixture into a pot.

Add in 1 cup water and stir well. Bring to a boil.

Take the pot off the heat and put in the teabag.

Let steep for 5 minutes.

nutrition (per serving): carbs: **9 g**, fat: **2.9 g**, protein: **3.1 g**, sodium: **47 mg**, sugars: **4.7 g**

pine needle tea

 1   20   31   9 g / 0.32 oz

you'll need:

1 small handful of fresh-picked pine needles, thoroughly washed

1 teaspoon sugar, or to taste

1/4 teaspoon dried lemon zest (optional)

on the trail:

Cut off any brown ends of the pine needles and chop them into small pieces to release juices and essential oils.

Bring 1 cup water to a boil in a pot.

Remove from the heat and add the needles, sugar, and lemon zest. Stir well.

Cover and steep for about 10 minutes.

Strain and enjoy.

* Cautions:

The potent mix of chemicals and active ingredients in pine can be dangerous for pregnant women.

Some varieties of pine can be poisonous, so always consult with a certified herbalist before picking needles in the wild.

baking on the trail

the outback oven

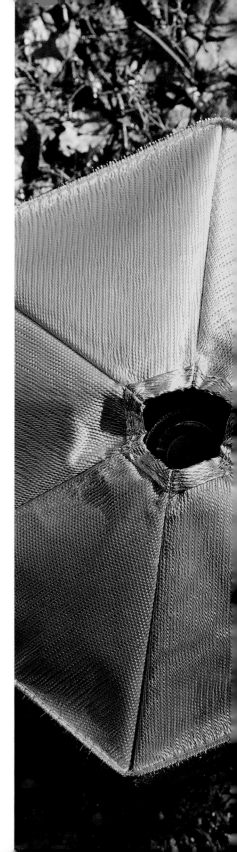

Are you dreaming about enjoying warm, freshly baked bread or muffins with a cup of tea or coffee on a cold morning in the backcountry? Just because you're hiking, doesn't mean you should forget about these treats.

The Outback Oven is a portable convection oven for baking while out in the wilderness. It is light enough to carry over short distances and compact enough to fit inside a backpack. With a little practice, you can make delicious pizzas, pies, cakes, lasagnas or casseroles – anything you can bake at home.

You can purchase this oven complete with a lid and non-stick frying pan, or use with your own lightweight cook set, which should be 10" in diameter or less. The Outback Oven kit also includes an 10" pot parka (convection dome), riser bar, scorch buster, reflector collar and a thermometer.

The Outback Oven requires little time to setup and bake (12–15 minutes) and can produce a perfect browned crust. However, it should be used only with stoves that are able to maintain a simmering function and the flame should be regulated very carefully. If the flame is too high, the food will burn on the bottom; if it's too low the food will be undercooked. Another drawback is that a windscreen is an essential while using the Outback Oven. Any significant wind can sharply increase cooking time.

how to bake

Pour the batter into an Outback Oven pan greased or lined with parchment paper. Silicone muffin cups are a good solution for trail baking too, as they are lightweight and very easy to clean.

Turn the stove on.

Place the ribbed heat diffuser plate on the stove's burner.

Set the pan on a riser bar and cover with a lid.

Adjust the oven thermometer on the pan lid.

Put the Pot Parka over the pan to hold the rising heat from the stove. The thermometer should be seen through an opening in the top of the Pot Parka. It has only three points: "Warm Up," "Bake," and "Burn."

Once the oven is heated, **set** the stove flame to minimum and maintain temperature in the "Bake" range until the food is ready.

Turn heat off. Let stand for 5 minutes.

* Cautions:

Do not use the Outback Oven with stoves that have burners mounted directly above their fuel source, as the heat may cause the fuel tank to over pressurize and rupture. Do not use an Outback Oven with a windscreen that encloses the fuel tank and stove together.

cinnamon snails

 4   60 241 254 g / 9.96 oz

you'll need:

Parchment paper

Dough:

1 cup all-purpose flour, plus extra for kneading

1/2 pack (about 5 g / 0.18 oz) dry yeast

1 tablespoon full cream milk powder

1 teaspoon sugar

Pinch of salt

1 teaspoon olive oil plus extra for greasing

Filling:

1/2 cup sugar

2 teaspoons ground cinnamon

at home:

Mix the flour, yeast, milk powder, sugar, and salt in a medium-sized zip lock bag.

Put the olive oil into a leak-proof container.

Combine the ingredients for the filling in another bag.

on the trail:

Pour 1/2 cup of lukewarm water and 1 teaspoon of olive oil into the bag with the flour mixture.

Knead the dough until smooth; then shape it into a ball.

Place the dough in a lightly greased pan.

Leave to rise for about 20 minutes or until it has doubled in size.

Stretch the dough into a rectangle.

Sprinkle with the filling mix.

Roll up the dough, seal the edges, and slice into 4–6 pieces.

Line an Oven pan with parchment paper and place in the prepared rolls.

Assemble the Outback Oven and bake for about 25 minutes.

Turn the heat off and let sit in the Oven for another 5 minutes.

nutrition (per serving): carbs: **52.3 g**, fat: **2.2 g**, protein: **4.4 g**, sodium: **49 mg,** sugars: **26.1 g**

chocolate muffins

 2   20   338   130 g / 4.59 oz

you'll need:

1 cup chocolate muffin mix

2 tablespoons olive oil

6 silicone (or paper) muffin cups

at home:

Pack the chocolate muffin mix in a medium-sized zip lock bag.

Put the olive oil into a leak-proof bottle.

on the trail:

Pour the olive oil and 2 tablespoons water (or more, if needed) into the bag with the dry baking mixture.

Seal the bag and knead the mixture until smooth.

Set muffin cups into an Oven pan.

Cut off a corner of the bag and squeeze batter into the muffin cups.

Assemble the Outback Oven and bake for about 12 minutes.

Turn the heat off and let sit in the Oven for another 5 minutes.

nutrition (per serving): carbs: **34.6 g**, fat: **21.7 g**, protein: **2.6 g**, sodium: **359 mg**, sugars: **17.9 g**

easy brownies

 4   30   Cal 525   409 g / 14.43 oz

you'll need:

1 cup all-purpose flour

1/2 cup sugar

2 tablespoons unsweetened cocoa powder

1/2 teaspoon baking powder

Small pinch of salt

1/2 cup olive oil

1/2 cup dark chocolate chips

Parchment paper

at home:

Mix the flour, sugar, cocoa, baking powder, and salt in a medium-sized zip lock bag.

Put the olive oil into a leak-proof container.

Pack the chocolate chips separately.

on the trail:

Pour the olive oil and 1/2 cup water (or more, if needed) into the bag with the dry brownie mixture.

Close the bag and knead until smooth.

Layer the Oven pan with parchment paper.

Cut off a corner of the bag and squeeze half of batter into the pan.

Sprinkle evenly with chocolate chips and fold the rest of the batter over.

Assemble the Outback Oven and bake for about 15 minutes.

Turn the heat off and let sit in the Oven for another 5 minutes.

nutrition (per serving): carbs: **60.6 g**, fat: **31.9 g**, protein: **4.8 g**, sodium: **75 mg**, sugars: **33.1 g**

backcountry blueberry cake

 4   30   336   295 g / 10.41 oz

you'll need:

2 cups all-purpose baking mix

1/4 cup olive oil

1 cup fresh-picked blueberries

Parchment paper

at home:

Pack the all-purpose baking mix in a medium-sized zip lock bag.

Put the olive oil into a leak-proof container.

on the trail:

Go and pick some fresh blueberries.

Pour the olive oil and 1/2 cup water (or more, if needed) into the bag with the dry baking mixture.

Close the bag and knead until smooth.

Layer the Oven pan with parchment paper.

Cut off a corner of the bag and squeeze half of batter into the pan.

Add half of the blueberries on top, spreading them evenly.

Pour over the rest of the batter and top with the remaining blueberries.

Assemble the Outback Oven and bake for about 12 minutes.

Turn the heat off and let sit in the Oven for another 5 minutes.

nutrition (per serving): carbs: **47.2 g**, fat: **15.3 g**, protein: **7.8 g**, sodium: **585 mg**, sugars: **6.6 g**

irish soda bread

 4   30   Cal 323   340 g / 12 oz

you'll need:

2 cups all-purpose flour, plus extra for kneading

1 tablespoon sugar

1/4 teaspoon baking soda

Pinch of salt

1/2 teaspoon baking powder

1/4 cup raisins

2 tablespoons full cream milk powder

1 teaspoon white wine vinegar or freshly squeezed lemon juice

1 tablespoon olive oil

Parchment paper

at home:

Mix the flour, sugar, soda, salt, baking powder, and raisins in a medium-sized zip lock bag.

Pack the remaining ingredients separately.

on the trail:

Combine the milk powder and 1/2 cup water in a mug.

Stir in the white wine vinegar. Let stand 5 minutes until the milk starts to curdle.

Pour the sour milk and olive oil into the bag with the dry soda bread mixture.

Using extra flour, gently **knead** the dough until smooth, and shape it into a ball.

Transfer the dough to an Oven pan lined with parchment paper.

Cut a shallow cross on the loaf's surface and dust it with flour.

Assemble the Outback Oven and bake for about 30 minutes.

Turn the heat off and let sit in the Oven for another 5 minutes.

nutrition (per serving): carbs: **60.2 g**, fat: **5.5 g**, protein: **7.9 g**, sodium: **139 mg**, sugars: **8.5 g**

drying food for the trail

Drying your own food for the trail is a great way to save money, lighten the weight of your backpack and enjoy quick, tasty and comforting meals throughout your adventure.

People who have never dehydrated food before are generally skeptical or cautious about doing it themselves, when in reality it is a simple, inexpensive process that can be done right at home. Once you start placing your first slices of food onto the dehydrator trays, you'll realize that it takes a lot less effort than you expected.

There are a wide variety of foods that your dehydrator can easily "dry out" such as fruits, meat, fish, and beans. It can even dehydrate entire meals as well as leftovers. By using the simple instructions provided in this book, you'll be able to make your own dried gourmet meals, even if you never thought it possible.

choosing a good food dehydrator

Modern food dehydrators now come in a variety of different shapes, sizes and price ranges. How do you choose one that will allow you to dry a large amount of food in the shortest period of time, and with no hassle?

There are five key factors to take into account while choosing a food dehydrator:

1. Wattage

More power means more efficiency and faster drying times. For best results choose a model with 400 watts or more.

2. Adjustable thermostat

This is one of the most important features of

a dehydrator. Since different foods require different temperatures for drying out, look for a model that has a thermostat with full temperature control from 40°C / 105°F to 74°C / 165°F.

3. Placement of fan and heating element

Placement of the fan and heating element

significantly impacts how quickly and how evenly your food will dry out. Models with a rear-mounted fan allow air to freely circulate across all the trays, which ensures a more even dry without the need for rotating racks.

4. Capacity

Adding extra trays for more capacity can expand the taller, stackable units. However, box models with square trays have up to 20% more drying space.

5. Timer and automatic shutoff

With these useful and handy functions, you can leave the dehydrator unattended while you sleep, walk or work. You can be confident that it will switch off after a certain drying period.

Recommendations:

You'll never go wrong if you choose an Excalibur dehydrator.

It's a bit pricey, but if you are serious about food dehydrating, it's worth the investment. You can choose among 4, 5 or 9-tray models, depending on your needs and budget.

I personally have a 9-tray Excalibur with a 26-hour timer and temperature control. It's fast, easy-to-use and jam-packed with special features. I can make a number of homemade treats, from banana chips to complete gourmet meals for backpacking.

fruits & berries

Pre-treat: Wash, peel, core, slice or shred your fruits.

To slow the browning process, some fruits such as bananas, apples, pears, and peaches should be dipped into an acid-citric bath (water with lemon juice, apple juice or pineapple juice) for a couple of minutes.

Canned fruits packed in water or juice should be drained before arranging on dehydrator trays.

Frozen fruits and berries require little or no pre-treatment.

Spread prepared fruits on dehydrator mesh sheets or trays covered with non-stick sheets or parchment paper in a single layer.

Dehydrate at 57°C / 135°F. Drying times* vary from plant to plant and depend largely on the sugar and water content of the food.

Store in airtight containers in a dark, cool place.

* Drying times for fruits and berries:

Food	Recommended pre-treatment	Drying time	Test
Apples	Peeling, slicing, dipping	7-15 hours	Pliable
Bananas	Peeling, slicing, dipping	6-10 hours	Leathery or crisp
Blueberries	Blanching	10-15 hours	Leathery
Citrus Fruits	Slicing	6-10 hours	Crisp
Cranberries	Blanching	10-15 hours	Pliable
Kiwifruit	Peeling, slicing	8-16 hours	Pliable
Mangoes	Peeling, slicing	8-16 hours	Pliable
Nectarines	Peeling, slicing, dipping	8-16 hours	Pliable
Peaches	Peeling, slicing, dipping	8-16 hours	Pliable
Pears	Slicing, peeling, dipping	8-16 hours	Pliable
Pineapple	Peeling, slicing	10-18 hours	Pliable
Rhubarb	Slicing, blanching	6-10 hours	Leathery
Strawberries	Slicing	8-16 hours	Leathery or crisp

vegetables

Pre-treat: Wash, peel, slice or shred your vegetables. Vegetables that have a relatively long cooking time such as broccoli, cauliflower, green beans, asparagus, pumpkin, and beets, should be steam-blanched or roasted before drying.

Spread prepared vegetables on dehydrator mesh sheets or trays covered with non-stick sheets or parchment paper in a single layer.

Dehydrate vegetables at 52°C / 130°F.

Store dried vegetables in airtight containers in a dark, cool place.

* Drying times for vegetables:

Food	Pre-Treatment	Drying time	Test
Asparagus	Slicing, peeling, blanching	5-6 hours	Brittle
Beans	Slicing, blanching	8-12 hours	Brittle
Beets	Cooking or baking, slicing	8-12 hours	Leathery
Broccoli	Slicing, blanching	10-14 hours	Brittle
Cabbages	Dipping, slicing, blanching	7-11 hours	Brittle
Carrots	Peeling, slicing, dipping, blanching	6-10 hours	Leathery
Cauliflower	Peeling, slicing, dipping, blanching	10-14 hours	Brittle
Eggplant	Peeling, slicing, dipping, roasting (optional)	4-8 hours	Leathery
Onions	Peeling, slicing	4-8 hours	Leathery
Peppers	Slicing	4-8 hours	Leathery
Potatoes	Peeling, slicing, dipping, blanching	6-14 hours	Brittle or leathery
Pumpkins	Peeling, slicing, cooking, baking or blanching	5-6 hours	Leathery
Tomatoes	Slicing, seeding (optional)	8-12 hours	Brittle or leathery
Zucchini	Peeling, slicing, dipping	6-10 hours	Brittle

* most drying times provided are from "Dehydration Guide", a booklet that accompanies the Excalibur dehydrator

mushrooms

Dehydrating mushrooms is a great way to preserve them for long-term storage or later use in backpacking meals. They are extremely lightweight, nutritious and very easy to rehydrate. Dried mushrooms can be used in soups, stews, omelets, pasta and many other dishes.

You can dehydrate nearly all edible mushrooms, like Chanterelles, Crimini, Enoki, Morels, Oyster Mushrooms, Porcini, Portobello and Shiitake.

Follow these steps to make your own dried mushrooms:

Clean the mushrooms: wash them and get all the dirt off using a brush or knife.

Slice the mushrooms: 6mm (1/4 inch) thick.

Arrange on dehydrator mesh sheets in a single layer.

Dehydrate at 54°C / 130°F for 4–8 hours or until completely dry and crispy.

Store dried mushrooms in airtight containers in a dark, cool place.

* Notes: To rehydrate mushrooms, just soak them in a cold or hot water for about 10–30 minutes. During this process, mushrooms will produce a dark, rich broth. Don't throw this out! Use this flavored soaking liquid for soup stocks and sauces.

canned meat

Place the canned meat into a saucepan and cook on low-to-medium heat until all gelatin/fat is melted.

Transfer meat to a colander and rinse it with hot, boiled water. Allow to cool. If necessary, pull the bigger chunks apart to make smaller pieces.

Spread the canned meat on dehydrator trays, covered with non-stick sheets or parchment paper.

Dehydrate at 68°C / 155°F for 4 to 8 hours until the meat is completely dry and hard.

Put into airtight containers, glass jars or zip lock bags.

Store in a dry, dark place at room temperature for two months. Vacuum-seal or freeze for a longer shelf life.

* Notes: Home-cooked chicken, whether it's been fried, grilled, poached or baked, is difficult to rehydrate. The best way to ensure that the chicken you dry turns out tender is to use pressure-cooked or canned chicken.

ground beef & turkey

Choose the leanest meat available. Put it in a skillet, break into fine pieces and cook until no pink meat remains.

Transfer meat to a colander to drain the fat. Rinse with hot, boiled water. Season to taste and leave to cool.

Spread cooked ground meat on dehydrator trays, covered with non-stick sheets or parchment paper.

Dehydrate at 68°C / 155°F for 4 to 6 hours until completely dry and brittle.

Put into airtight containers, glass jars or zip lock bags.

Store in a dry, dark place at room temperature for two months. Vacuum-seal or freeze for a longer shelf life.

how to make jerky

Choose a lean cut of meat in excellent condition. Most meat, including poultry and game, can be successfully dried into jerky.

Trim the visible fat off and throw out any filmy membrane tissue.

Cut into thin strips or slices, about 6mm (1/4 inch).

Marinate for 6–12 hours in the refrigerator.

Pre-cook meat by either roasting or steaming them to get an inner temperature 71–74°C / 160–165°F. This step ensures that any bacteria present will be destroyed before drying.

Rinse off and spread on dehydrator trays.

Dehydrate at 68°C / 155°F temperature for 4–6 hours until hard and no moisture pockets available. Meat should be dry-leathery or partly brittle when done.

Put into vacuum-sealed containers, glass jars or zip lock bags.

Store in a dry, dark place at room temperature for two weeks.

fish jerky

Always use only fresh lean fish that was not frozen for the highest quality jerky. Cod, halibut, bass and sole are some types of lean fish to choose from. Fatty or oily fish spoil rapidly.

Skin and bone the fish.

Cut into thin strips or slices, about 6mm (1/4 inch).

Marinate for 6–12 hours in the refrigerator.

Rinse and spread on dehydrator trays.

Dehydrate at 68°C / 155°F for 8 to 12 hours. When done, the fish jerky should be a little brittle or dry-leathery.

Put dried fish into airtight containers, glass jars or zip lock bags.

Store in a dry, dark place at room temperature for two weeks.

canned / frozen seafood

You can also dehydrate pouched, canned or pre-cooked frozen seafood. Tuna in water, shrimp, mussels and imitation crabmeat are tasty foods that can easily be rehydrated while on the trail.

Drain all liquid from the can. Thaw out frozen products in refrigerator.

Pull fish/seafood chunks apart into tiny pieces.

Spread fish or seafood pieces on dehydrator trays, covered with non-stick sheets or parchment paper.

Dehydrate at 68°C / 155°F for 4 to 8 hours until completely dry and hard.

Put dried fish into airtight containers, glass jars or zip lock bags.

Store in a dry, dark place at room temperature for two months. Vacuum-seal or freeze for longer shelf life.

pasta

Choose smaller and shorter varieties of pasta. They take less space compared to long shape sorts like spaghetti or angel hair. Furthermore, long shape pasta is hard to bag, as it has very sharp ends that can damage packaging.

Cook your pasta in salted boiling water according to package instructions.

Drain water off. Rinse pasta with cold water to stop the cooking process.

Spread the cooked pasta on dehydrator mesh sheets or lined trays (for small pasta shapes) in a single layer.

Dry at 57°C / 135°F for about 2–4 hours until hard.

Put dried pasta into vacuum-sealed containers, jars or zip lock bags.

Store in a dry, dark place at room temperature.

Why have you to dehydrate pasta if it's already dried?

There are three key reasons:

- First, dehydrated pasta can be done very quickly (rehydrates in 2–3 minutes in boiling water), saving both time and fuel on the trail.

- Second, you can cook it without draining water off.

- And finally, you can mix dehydrated pasta together with other foods like dried meat and powdered sauces to create one-pot backpacking meals.

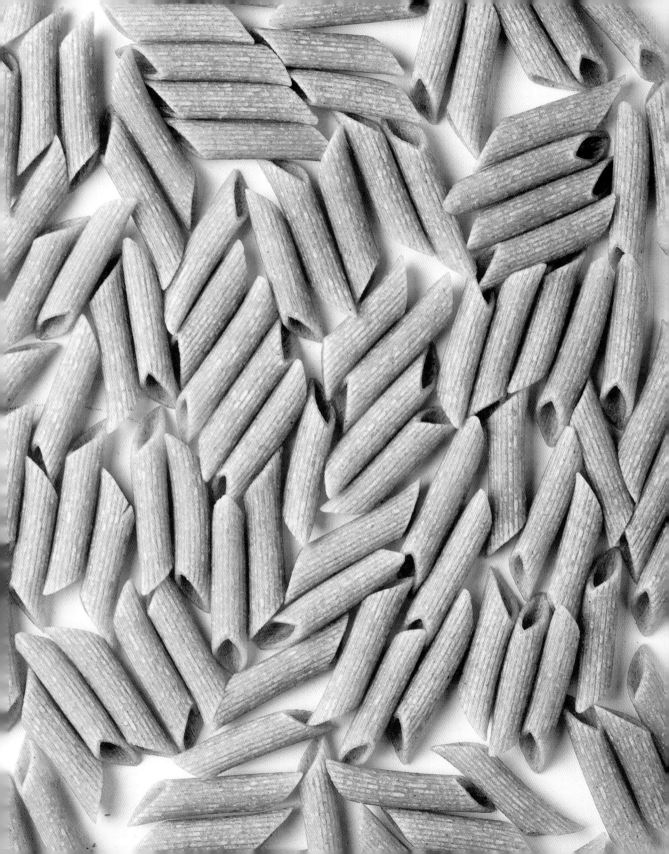

canned beans & lentils

Place legumes in a colander, drain and rinse well.

Spread on dehydrator trays covered with non-stick sheets or parchment paper.

Dry at 55°C / 130°F for 4–6 hours.

Put dried pulses (legumes) into vacuum-sealed containers, jars or zip lock bags.

Store in a dry, dark place at room temperature.

* Notes: Home cooked dried beans can stay hard and don't rehydrate as quickly as canned beans and lentils.

cooked grains

Whole grains, not the ones that are quick or instant, contain many important nutrients, but they are very slow cooking. In order to save yourself time and fuel on the trail, it's best to dehydrate them at home.

Place grains in a colander. Rinse with warm water 2–3 times.

Fold into salted, boiling water. Stir well. Reduce heat to low and simmer for 10–30 minutes, or until ready.

Take off the heat, drain excess water and allow to cool.

Spread cooked grains on dehydrator trays covered with non-stick sheets or parchment paper in an even, thin layer.

Dry grains at 55°C / 130°F for 3–6 hours until brittle.

Put dried grains into vacuum-sealed containers, jars or zip lock bags.

Store in a dry, dark place at room temperature.

whole meals & leftovers

There are two ways to prepare dehydrated backpacking meals

- when you make the meal, by assembling the powdered and/or dried ingredients or

- by cooking the entire meal first, then dehydrating it.

Both methods are good; however, to successfully dehydrate whole meals and leftovers you have to follow some rules:

Thoroughly **cook** your food before it's placed in the dehydrator.

Always **reheat** leftovers before drying, to prevent the growth of bacteria.

Cut or shred your vegetables, fish and meats into smaller pieces. This ensures quicker drying and faster rehydration when you're at the campsite.

Place the food evenly on the dehydrator so it quickly dries the food out.

Allow the dehydrated food to cool down before you package it.

Divide and pack meals into single servings.

Label and date each bag.

Store bags with dried food in a cool, dry, dark place, preferably in the freezer.

Do not dry food that contains oils, fats and dairy products. It will likely become rancid quickly.

rehydration basics

The general rule for food rehydration is to use equal parts water and dried food (1 cup of dried meal to 1 cup of water). You can always add more water later to get the consistency you want. How long it'll take your food to rehydrate will depend on a number of factors:

The size of the piece of food. Smaller pieces of food and powders rehydrate almost instantly. Larger pieces may take from 30 minutes to several hours.

The type of food and whether it was fresh, cooked or canned before drying. Uncooked food takes longer to rehydrate than roasted, canned or blanched food.

The degree of dryness of the food. Food that was dehydrated until hard will take more time to rehydrate.

The temperature of liquid being used to rehydrate the food. You can use both cold and hot water for this process. However, rehydration with hot water and further cooking work best for the trail.

dehydrated food recipes

banana chips

 3   -   115   33 g / 1.16 oz

you'll need:

2–3 ripe bananas (not overripe), peeled

1 tablespoon fresh pressed lemon juice

at home:

Cut the bananas into 3–4 mm (1/8 inch) slices.

Mix the lemon juice with 1/4 cup water in a mug.

Place the banana slices on a dehydrator tray.

Brush each slice on both sides with the mix of lemon juice and water.

Dehydrate at 57°C / 135°F for 6–10 hours until crisp.

Store in an airtight container in a dark, dry place.

nutrition (per serving): carbs: **29.4 g**, fat: **0.6 g**, protein: **1.3 g**, sodium: **1 mg,** sugars: **15.8 g**

applesauce leather rolls

 4   -   **Cal** 122   21 g / 1.48 oz

you'll need:

4 apples, peeled, cored and roughly chopped

1/2 cup apple juice

1 tablespoon freshly squeezed lemon juice

1 tablespoon sugar

1/4 teaspoon ground cinnamon

at home:

Put the apples into a large saucepan.

Pour in the apple juice and lemon juice.

Place over medium heat and bring to a boil.

Add the sugar and cinnamon, and stir well.

Reduce heat to low, put a lid on and simmer until the apples are tender, for about 15–20 minutes.

Remove from the heat and cool to room temperature.

Purée the apples using a hand blender or food processor.

Spread the purée on dehydrator trays covered with non-stick sheets or parchment paper.

Dehydrate at 57°C / 135°F for 10–12 hours until pliable.

Cut into strips and roll.

Store in an airtight container in a dark, dry place.

nutrition (per serving): carbs: **31.9 g**, fat: **0.4 g**, protein: **0.6 g**, sodium: **3 mg**, sugars: **25.4 g**

thai style beef jerky

 3   -   249   38 g / 1.34 oz

you'll need:

300 g / 0.66 lb lean cut of beef

For marinade:

1/2 cup light soy sauce

1/2 cup freshly squeezed orange juice

1 tablespoon brown sugar

2 garlic cloves, minced

1 teaspoon ground fresh ginger

at home:

Trim off any excess fat and silverskin from the beef.

Place the beef in a zip lock bag and freeze for about 2 hours until firm.

Remove meat from the freezer and cut into 6 mm (1/8 inch) strips.

In a bowl, **combine** all the ingredients for the marinade.

Add the beef to the marinade and stir well to coat each slice.

Cover and refrigerate for 6–8 hours.

Then, **take out** the meat and drain it in a colander.

Place beef slices on a dehydrator tray.

Dry at 71–74°C / 160–165°F for 1 hour, then reduce temperature to 68°C / 155°F and continue to dry until pliable, with no moisture pockets visible (about 5–7 hours).

Store in an airtight container in a dark, dry place.

nutrition (per serving): carbs: **13.2 g**, fat: **6.4 g**, protein: **33.1 g**, sodium: **1485 mg**, sugars: **7.3 g**

unstuffed peppers

 4   20   684   130 g / 4.59 oz

you'll need:

1 tablespoon olive oil

1 onion, chopped

2 garlic cloves, minced

600 g / 1.3 lb lean beef mince

3 green bell peppers, chopped

1 can (400 g / 14 oz.) diced tomatoes

Salt, to taste

Sugar, to taste

1 teaspoon of dried basil

1 teaspoon of dried oregano

2 cups cooked rice

at home:

Heat the olive oil in a large saucepan over medium-low heat Gently **fry** the onion and garlic for about 3 minutes, stirring regularly.

Add the ground beef and cook until fully brown. **Transfer** the meat to a colander. **Drain** and then return it to the saucepan.

Tip in the green pepper and continue to cook for about 5 minutes.

Stir in the diced tomatoes and dried herbs. **Bring** to a boil and season to taste. **Reduce** heat to low, put a lid on and leave to cook for a further 10 minutes.

Add the cooked rice and simmer for a couple of minutes together. Then, **remove** from the heat and let cool thoroughly.

Spread the unstuffed pepper mixture on dehydrator trays covered with non-stick sheets or parchment paper.

Dehydrate at 63°C / 145°F for 8–10 hours until brittle.

Divide the dried meal into equal portions (about 1 cup each) and pack them into separate zip lock bags.

on the trail:

To rehydrate 1 portion:

Put the dried meal in a pot and add 1 cup water.

Bring to a boil and cook, stirring occasionally, for about 10–15 minutes, until rehydrated.

nutrition (per serving): carbs: **97.8 g**, fat: **13.6 g**, protein: **41.8 g**, sodium: **603 mg**, sugars: **14.8 g**

three mushroom risotto

 1   20 669 147 g / 5.19 oz

you'll need:

1/2 cup dehydrated cooked rice

1/2 cup dried mushroom mix (porcini, portobello, and cremini)

1/4 vegetable bouillon cube, crushed

1/2 teaspoon dried parsley

1/4 teaspoon dried thyme

Salt, to taste

Pepper, to taste

2 tablespoons grated Parmesan cheese

at home:

Mix the rice, mushrooms, bouillon cube, and dried herbs in a zip lock bag.

Pack the remaining ingredients separately.

on the trail:

Put the dried meal in a pot and add 1 cup water.

Stir well, cover, and let soak for 5 minutes.

Place the pot over medium heat and bring to a boil. Season to taste.

Cook, stirring occasionally, for about 10 minutes, until rehydrated.

Serve topped with Parmesan cheese.

nutrition (per serving): carbs: **117.3 g**, fat: **7.2 g**, protein: **25.7 g**, sodium: **596 mg**, sugars: **0 g**

penne puttanesca

 4   20 445 135 g / 4.76 oz

you'll need:

4 cups whole wheat penne pasta

1 tablespoon olive oil

3 garlic cloves, finely chopped

1 smal red onion, diced

6-8 anchovy fillets

1 can (about 800 g / 14 oz) diced tomatoes

2 tablespoons capers

1/4 cup Gaeta or Kalamata olives, pitted and roughly chopped

Salt

Sugar

8 tablespoons grated Parmesan cheese (2 tablespoons per portion)

at home:

Cook the pasta in salted boiling water according to package instructions. Once cooked, **rinse** pasta under cold water to stop the cooking process. **Drain** and set aside.

Heat the olive oil in a saucepan over medium heat. Gently **fry** the onion and garlic for about 3 minutes, stirring regularly. **Add** the anchovies and cook, stirring regularly, until melted.

Stir in the diced tomatoes, capers and olives. **Season** to taste with salt and sugar. **Reduce** heat to low, put a lid on and leave to simmer for 10 minutes, until sauce is slightly thickened. **Remove** from the heat and cool thoroughly.

Spread the pasta and sauce on separate dehydrator trays covered with non-stick sheets or parchment paper.

Dehydrate at 57°C / 134°F for 2–4 hours until pasta has dried. Then, take the trays with pasta off from the dehydrator and dry the sauce for another 4–8 hours until hard and brittle.

Divide the dried sauce and pasta into equal portions and pack them into separate zip lock bags.

Pack Parmesan cheese separately.

on the trail:

Put the dried meal in a pot and add 1 cup water.

Bring to a boil and cook, stirring occasionally, for about 10–15 minutes, until rehydrated.

Serve topped with grated Parmesan cheese.

nutrition (per serving): carbs: **56.8 g**, fat: **16.1 g**, protein: **23.8 g**, sodium: **1430 mg**, sugars: **10.4 g**

trail chili

 4   20 681 150 g / 5.29 oz

you'll need:

1 tablespoon olive oil

1 red onion, chopped

2 cloves garlic, minced

600 g / 1.3 lb lean beef mince

2 red bell peppers, chopped

1 can (400 g / 14 oz.) kidney beans, drained

1 can (340 g / 12 oz) sweetcorn, drained

2 tablespoons chili con carne spice mixture

1 can (400 g / 14 oz.) diced tomatoes

Salt, to taste

Sugar, to taste

at home:

Heat the olive oil in a saucepan over medium heat. Gently **fry** the onion and garlic for about 3 minutes, stirring regularly.

Add the ground beef and cook until fully brown. **Transfer** the meat to a colander. **Drain** and then return to the saucepan.

Tip in the red pepper, beans, sweetcorn, and chili con carne spice mixture.

Continue to cook for about 5 minutes, stirring occasionally.

Pour in the diced tomatoes together with their juice and bring to a boil. Season. **Reduce** heat to low, put a lid on, and leave to cook for a further 10 minutes.

Remove from the heat and cool thoroughly.

Spread the trail chili mixture on dehydrator trays covered with non-stick sheets or parchment paper.

Dehydrate at 63°C / 145°F for 8–12 hours until brittle.

Divide the dried meal into equal portions (about 1 cup each) and pack them into separate zip lock bags.

on the trail:

To rehydrate 1 portion:

Put the dried meal in a pot and add 1 cup water.

Bring to a boil and cook, stirring occasionally, for about 10–15 minutes, until rehydrated.

---

nutrition (per serving): carbs: **88.2 g**, fat: **13 g**, protein: **58.1 g**, sodium: **90 mg**, sugars: **11.2 g**

vegan bulgur chili

 4   15 600 115 g / 4.06 oz

you'll need:

1 tablespoon olive oil

1 red onion, chopped

1 red bell pepper, chopped

1 can (400 g / 14 oz.) diced tomatoes

1 cup vegetable stock

3/4 cup quick-cooking bulgur

1 teaspoon Mexican seasoning

Salt, to taste

Sugar, to taste

1 can (400 g / 14 oz.) kidney beans, drained

4 pieces dark chocolate (70% cacao)

at home:

Heat the olive oil in a saucepan over medium heat. Gently **cook** the onion, stirring regularly, until softened.

Stir in the red bell peppers, bulgur, and Mexican seasoning. **Heat** together for a couple of minutes.

Pour in the diced tomatoes and vegetable stock; bring to a boil. Season to taste with salt and sugar.

Add the kidney beans and simmer for 6–7 minutes, until the bulgur is tender and almost all the liquid is absorbed.

Remove from the heat and cool to room temperature.

Spread the bulgur chili mixture on dehydrator trays covered with non-stick sheets or parchment paper.

Dehydrate at 52°C / 125°F for 8–10 hours until brittle.

Divide the dried meal into equal portions (about 1 cup each) and pack them into separate zip lock bags.

Pack chocolate pieces separately.

on the trail:

To rehydrate 1 portion:

Put the dried meal in a pot and add 1 cup water.

Bring to a boil and cook, stirring occasionally, for about 10–15 minutes, until rehydrated.

Stir in chocolate pieces and enjoy!

---

nutrition (per serving): carbs: **106 g**, fat: **8.4 g**, protein: **29.8 g**, sodium: **110 mg**, sugars: **12.4 g**

pappardelle bolognese

 4   15   691   115 g / 4.06 oz

you'll need:

340 g / 12 oz pappardelle pasta

1 tablespoon olive oil

1 onion, finely diced

2 carrots, peeled and finely diced

1 celery stalk, finely diced

2 garlic cloves, minced

600 g / 1.3 lb lean beef mince

1 can (400 g / 14 oz.) diced tomatoes

1 cup vegetable stock

Salt, to taste

Sugar, to taste

1 teaspoon dried basil

1 teaspoon dried oregano

8 tablespoons grated Parmesan cheese (2 tablespoons per portion)

at home:

Cook the pasta in salted boiling water according to package instructions. Once cooked, **rinse** pasta under cold water to stop the cooking process. **Drain** and set aside.

Heat the olive oil in a saucepan over medium heat. Gently **fry** onions, carrot, celery, and garlic until they have softened.

Add the minced beef and cook, stirring occasionally, until fully brown. **Transfer** the meat to a colander. **Drain** and then return it to the saucepan.

Stir in the diced tomatoes, vegetable stock, and dried herbs. **Season** to taste with salt and sugar. **Reduce** heat to low, put a lid on and leave to simmer for 20 minutes, until sauce is well reduced. **Remove** from the heat and cool thoroughly.

Spread the pasta and sauce on separate dehydrator trays.

Dehydrate at 57°C / 134°F for 2–4 hours until pasta has dried. Then, turn the heat up to 63°C / 145°F and dry the sauce for another 6–8 hours until hard and brittle.

Divide the dried sauce and pasta into equal portions (about 1 cup each) and pack them into separate zip lock bags.

Pack Parmesan cheese separately.

on the trail:

Put the dried meal in a pot and add 1 cup water.

Bring to a boil and cook, stirring occasionally, for about 10 minutes, until rehydrated. Serve topped with grated Parmesan cheese.

nutrition (per serving): carbs: **72.9 g**, fat: **15.4 g**, protein: **59.4 g**, sodium: **208 mg**, sugars: **7.4 g**

soba and veggies stir-fry

 1   15   Cal 396   104 g / 3.67 oz

you'll need:

1 tablespoon dehydrated red bell peppers

1 tablespoon dehydrated mushrooms

1 tablespoon dehydrated pak choi leaves (Chinese cabbage)

1 bundle (about 60 g / 2 oz.) soba noodles

1 teaspoon chili sauce

1 teaspoon light soy sauce

1 teaspoon fish sauce

at home:

Combine dehydrated vegetables and mushrooms in a zip lock bag.

Mix all sauces in a small leak-proof bottle.

Pack soba noodles separately.

on the trail:

Put the dried vegetable and mushroom mixture into a pot and add 1 cup water.

Place the pot over medium heat and bring to a boil.

Cook for about 5 minutes, stirring occasionally.

Add the noodles and cook together for another 5 minutes until ready.

Remove from the heat and drain off the excess water.

Pour in the sauce mix and stir well.

nutrition (per serving): carbs: **23.3 g**, fat: **18.4 g**, protein: **39.3 g**, sodium: **178 mg**, sugars: **13.6 g**

moussaka casserole

 4   20   Cal 396   100 g / 3.53 oz

you'll need:

1 medium eggplant, roughly chopped

1 green bell pepper, chopped

1 red bell pepper, chopped

2 tomatoes, chopped

Salt, to taste

2 tablespoons olive oil, divided

1 onion, diced

2 garlic cloves, finely chopped

600 g / 1.3 lb lean beef mince

1 can (400 g / 14 oz.) diced tomatoes

1 handful fresh chopped parsley

Pepper, to taste

Sugar, to taste

at home:

Heat the oven to 200°C / 400°F. Line a baking sheet with parchment paper.

Place the eggplant, peppers and tomatoes on prepared baking sheet.

Season with salt and drizzle evenly with 1 tablespoon of olive oil.

Roast for about 20–30 minutes until tender.

Meanwhile, **heat** the remaining olive oil in a saucepan over medium heat.

Gently **fry** the onion and garlic for about 3 minutes, stirring regularly.

Add the ground beef and cook until fully brown.

Transfer the meat to a colander. **Drain** and then return meat to the saucepan.

Stir in the diced tomatoes, roasted vegetables and dried parsley. **Season**.

Turn heat to low, put a lid on, and leave to simmer for a further 5 minutes.

Remove from the heat and cool thoroughly.

nutrition (per serving): carbs: **23.3 g**, fat: **18.4 g**, protein: **39.3 g**, sodium: **178 mg**, sugars: **13.6 g**

Spread the moussaka on dehydrator trays covered with non-stick sheets or parchment paper.

Dehydrate at 63°C / 145°F for 8–10 hours until brittle.

Divide the dried moussaka mixture to equal portions (about 1 cup each) and pack them into separate zip lock bags.

on the trail:

To rehydrate 1 portion:

Put the dried meal in a pot and add 1 cup water.

Bring to a boil and cook, stirring occasionally, for about 10–15 minutes, until rehydrated.

vegetable yellow curry

 1   20 404 85 g / 3 oz

you'll need:

1/3 cup basmati rice

1 teaspoon Thai yellow curry paste

1 cup frozen vegetable mix

2 tablespoons coconut milk powder

at home:

Cook rice in salted boiling water according to package instructions.

Drain and cool slightly.

Spread the rice, vegetables, and curry paste on separate dehydrator trays, covered with non-stick sheets or parchment paper.

Dry at 57°C / 135°F for 4–8 hours.

Combine all the ingredients in a medium-sized zip lock bag.

on the trail:

Put the dried meal in a pot and add 1 cup water.

Bring to a boil and cook, stirring occasionally, for about 10–15 minutes, until rehydrated.

nutrition (per serving): carbs: **66.6 g**, fat: **10.6 g**, protein: **7.8 g**, sodium: **176 mg**, sugars: **5.1 g**

"ant-hill"

 1   20   Cal 331   119 g / 4.20 oz

you'll need:

60 g / 2 oz rice noodles

1/4 cup dehydrated beef mince

1 teaspoon dehydrated grated ginger

1 teaspoon dehydrated red chili (seeded and sliced)

2 tablespoons dehydrated green bell pepper

1 teaspoon sesame oil

1 tablespoon soy sauce

1/2 teaspoon sesame seeds

at home:

Combine the rice noodles, dehydrated meat, and dried vegetables in a zip lock bag.

Mix the sesame oil and soy sauce in a small leak-proof bottle.

Pack the sesame seeds separately.

on the trail:

Put the dried meal in a pot and add 1 cup water.

Bring to a boil and cook, stirring occasionally, for about 10–15 minutes, until rehydrated.

Pour in the sauce mix and stir well.

Sprinkle with sesame seeds and serve.

nutrition (per serving): carbs: **20.8 g**, fat: **13.1 g**, protein: **34.3 g**, sodium: **1014 mg**, sugars: **2.8 g**

"honolulu" curry

 1   20 Cal 636 102 g / 3.60 oz

you'll need:

1/3 cup dehydrated basmati rice

2 tablespoons dehydrated shrimp

2 tablespoons dehydrated canned pineapples

1 teaspoon mild curry powder

2 tablespoons coconut milk powder

at home:

Mix all the ingredients in a medium-sized zip lock bag.

on the trail:

Put the dried meal in a pot and add 1 cup water.

Bring to a boil and cook, stirring occasionally, for about 10–15 minutes, until rehydrated.

nutrition (per serving): carbs: **60.9 g**, fat: **33.4 g**, protein: **25.5 g**, sodium: **352 mg**, sugars: **3.2 g**

food planning

how to get food organized for a multi-day trip

Considering "what you are going to eat" is an important part of preparing for a multi-day trip in the wilderness. Well-balanced, carefully planned food will allow you to enjoy quick, easy, great tasting and nutritious meals on the trail. This step-by-step guide will help you create your own backpacking menu and arrange food for your adventures in the great outdoors.

Pick your favourite recipes. Flip through your favourite books or check out the Internet and pick some recipes you really like. Look at the nutrition facts, weight of the ingredients, the gear you'll need and cooking skills required.

Build a meal planning form. Figure out how many days you'll be on the trail, and then count the number of meals you'll need in each category (breakfast, lunch, dinner, snacks). Create a meal planning form and write down recipes you've collected for each day of your trip.

Make your food list. Identify all ingredients needed for your backpacking menu. Write a food list that will make your grocery shopping easier and faster.

Go shopping. When shopping at the grocery store, stick to your food list so that you don't forget crucial ingredients or buy things you don't need.

Do all "at home" jobs. Follow "at home" directions for selected backpacking recipes. For dehydrated meals, do all the necessary pre-treatment, cooking and drying.

Bag, seal and mark. Pack your dried meals, prepared ingredients and snacks in sealable plastic bags. Don't forget to include "on the trail" cooking instructions for each bag. You can write these directly on the bags or tuck in printed instructions.

Arrange your food. Group packed meals by the day they should be consumed or by meal course. Pack and clearly label each group separately to make sure you know where everything is and can get to it when needed.

Pack your backpack. Put all your grouped meals in one waterproof bag, stuff sack or bear canister. Don't forget to include your spices and condiments. Use a separate bag if you need to pack kitchen utensils for the trail.

How much food to take?

It's very personal and depends on factors like your age, gender, body size and physical activity level. Usually 1 – 1.5 pounds (500–900g) of food per day is enough to meet the caloric needs of 2500–3000 calories for one person in moderate backpacking, ski touring or paddling trip.

For strenuous activities, recommended daily intake is 3000–3700 calories.

In extreme mountaineering and in colder weather trips, you'll burn a lot of calories just to stay warm, so pack accordingly and increase calorie consumption up to 3700–4500 calories.

5-day menu plan

Here is a complete 5-day lightweight backpacking meal plan that I have used in my own adventures on different trails. This menu will feed one outdoorsman with an average appetite. It includes three main meals (breakfast, lunch, dinner) and two snacks providing **2374 calories** from **547g / 1.21 lb** of food per day.

Total weight of food: **2.73 kg / 6.03 lb**

You can easily add another 1–2k calories to the daily plan by doubling up on the snacks or by increasing portion sizes.

DAY 1	Weight of food: 566 g / 1.25 lb; Caloric value: 2518 Cal
Breakfast:	Oatmeal With Bacon and Honey, Really Hot Chocolate
Lunch:	Harira Soup, Whole Wheat Tortilla
Snack 1:	Puffed Amaranth and Peanut Butter Bar
Snack 2:	Thai Style Beef Jerky
Dinner:	Pappardelle Bolognese, After Dinner Tea
DAY 2	Weight of food: 501 g / 1.10 lb; Caloric value: 2293 Cal
Breakfast:	Superfood Granola, Pina Colada Latte
Lunch:	Chanterelle and Lentil Soup
Snack 1:	Dried Fruit Salami
Snack 2:	Spicy Roasted Nuts and Seeds
Dinner:	Unstuffed Peppers, Good Night Tea

DAY 3	Weight of food: 665 g / 1.47 lb; Caloric value: 2559 Cal
Breakfast:	Creamy Chocolate Buckwheat, Cacao Drink
Lunch:	Curried Ramen Bowl, Whole Wheat Tortilla
Snack 1:	Cornflake Energy Bar
Snack 2:	Thai Style Beef Jerky
Dinner:	Penne Puttanesca, Easy Trail Tiramisu
DAY 4	Weight of food: 590 g / 1.30 lb; Caloric value: 2525 Cal
Breakfast:	Granola with Hazelnuts and Dark Chocolate, Halva Coffee
Lunch:	Miso Soup With Tortellini
Snack 1:	Spicy Roasted Nuts and Seeds
Snack 2:	Puffed Amaranth and Peanut Butter Bar
Dinner:	Trail Chili, Dried Fruit Compote
DAY 5	Weight of food: 412 g / 0.90 lb; Caloric value: 1979 Cal
Breakfast:	Peanut Butter Couscous, Really Hot Chocolate
Lunch:	Creamy Mushroom Soup
Snack 1:	Cornflake Energy Bar
Snack 2:	No Bake Energy Bites
Dinner:	Honolulu Curry, Masala Chai

index